Coffee and Cake

Coffee and Cake

– An Adoptee –
in Search of Her Past

BY *Julia I. Meyers*

Acclaim Press
MORLEY, MISSOURI

Acclaim Press
— Your Next Great Book —
P.O. Box 238
Morley, MO 63767
(573) 472-9800
www.acclaimpress.com

Library of Congress Cataloging-in-Publication Data

Meyers, Julia I.
Coffee and cake: an adoptee in search of her past / by Julia I. Meyers.
p. cm.
ISBN-13: 978-1-935001-57-7 (alk. paper)
ISBN-10: 1-935001-57-4 (alk. paper)
1. Meyers, Julia I. 2. Meyers, Julia I.--Family. 3. Adoptees--United States--Biography. 4. Identity (Psychology)--United States--Case studies. 5. Intercountry adoption--Case studies. 6. Family reunions--Case studies. 7. Birthmothers--Germany--Biography. 8. Birthfathers--United States--Biography. 9. Germany--Biography. I. Title.
HV874.82.M49A3 2010
362.734092--dc22
[B]

2010032141

First Printing: 2010
Printed in the United States of America
10 9 8 7 6 5 4 3 2 1

Contents

Dedicated to my parents,
all four of them!

In Memoriam of
Jennifer Lynn Hoffmann
Who will never be forgotten

Introduction

My name is Julia Isabell Meyers and I was born in Germany in 1968. At two months of age I was adopted by my loving parents and grew up with one younger adopted brother in a small, picturesque German community.

This book begins with the rather sudden decision at age 28 to contact my birth mother. Finding her was the easy part, but writing the letter proved an emotional roller coaster and took eight months. I was aware that this one letter would be a life-changing event to a women I did not know. In fact, Edda, my birth mother, never forgot about the baby she gave away and always longed for my return. She answered that she could not wait to meet with me. By shear coincidence, the day of our reunion was emotionally amplified with the startling and agonizing rejected-love, motivated murder of my friend. In one day, a daughter was found and another one lost.

After our meeting, the buried complications of our new relationship began to unfold in 207 letters exchanged over two continents. The letters slowly revealed the silent pain of a mother's twenty-eight-year-old decision to selflessly sever a part of herself as a gift to strangers. Does time and space really separate a mother and child? Since the separation, Edda's every major life event was re-examined with nostalgia. What if things had been different and Edda hadn't given away her baby? Would we still be together and share everything? Where was I now? What was I doing? Was I loved? Her Baby. Her Daughter. Her Love. Can the power of love and longing bring a baby back? And for me the question arose: can an adult woman fill the void of having lost a baby so many years prior?

The answer was an unforeseeable mixture of all possibilities that led me to the edge of identity crisis when confronted with my three half sisters. My birth mother had even giving the last of her three other daughters the same name: Christine. Was I still as singular as I thought when I subsequently got to know them and found out how many inner and outer features we had in common.

New relationships were born. My sister's birth order and established roles had to be reorganized according to the new situation. My birth mother's heart was only briefly whole because her husband denied complete acknowledgement of motherhood. Instead of resolution, I inadvertently stirred up disorientation, old pain, and new conflicts.

Our fragile relationship developed slowly, not as a mother and daughter, but as something in-between friendship and heredity was yet to be defined. As a woman with a devoted family of my own, I could not bring back Edda's lost baby and the years between. Can a woman truly be a daughter to two mothers? This question gains a new meaning when I marry and have children on my own, which changed my perspective as a daughter to that of a mother.

Curiosity, resentment and lost love are the conflicting signals sent by my birth mother along with the photograph and name; Ottie Garrett. Yet, requesting that I not look for him. Finally, the shared curiosity of mother and daughter overrides our fear of the unknown. A thirty-year-old, black and white, ½ by ½ inch photo of an American soldier, hidden away in Germany, links me to my birth father and led to finding him.

The publication of an autobiography by my birth father's Amish wife reflects the turning point in the decision to contact the last missing link of my past. In the biography, Ottie's wife, Ruth Irene, describes her childhood with the Amish and her escape with him. Her loving description of Ottie determined my decision to write the second life changing letter, this time to my American birth father. The letter was composed with the help of two of my half-sisters, curious of their mother's life prior to her marriage to their father. Delayed through some misfortunate events a response finally arrives.

Overwhelming feelings of joy, fear, and unexpected relief overcame me. The unanticipated warm acceptance by my birth father seemed almost unbearable and a first meeting is stalled by me. In contrast to my birth mother where circumstances were difficult and the physical separation through an ocean slowed down the process of familiarity, Ottie does not rest until he could first visit his newfound daughter in the backdrop of the American Southwest. And only a few months later he properly introduces me, my husband and children to his entire extended family and friends in his home state of Kentucky.

My identity is questioned once again, now as a new family claims my personality and physical appearance as resemblance of their own heritage. I was confronted a second time with the profound question of what is a family and how to define myself as an individual. I realize that for myself the definition of family is fourfold: in the center is my own husband and two young children and my parents and brother in Germany. These two core families which present familiarity and stability are amplified by the loving relationship of my two newly found birth families.

I wrote this book, because I know this story is unique. I am very lucky that despite some problems, I was welcomed warmly by all the people I had encountered and that my parents were so understanding with my decision to venture into my past.

I have known many people who were adopted, have adopted, or have given for adoption. In a few cases the children tried to find their birth parents, many times they either did not find them or were very disappointed. I have also known several cases where children did not know they were adopted until they were older. It almost always ended in a disaster and the trust between the child and the parents had been permanently damaged. I was fortunate that my parents had always told us and being adopted had been rather fun for us, it was cool and not strange.

My wish is that this book can provide some sort of comfort and hope for people involved in adoption of any kind. Adoption is a wonderful thing, it gives parents who otherwise can not have children the possibility of having children, it gives children without parents a home.

I have changed several names of the main characters in this book in order to protect the identity of the described. I would like to mention that this book is written solely based on my memories and the letters, Edda and I exchanged. If I have misinterpreted or misrepresented events I apologize. This is how I remember the events which spanned over eleven years of my life from making the decision to find my birth mother in January 1996 to taking my birth father's wife Irene to meet Edda in Germany in November 2007. I hope this book can inspire you to accept the variety of your own family, to see them as individuals and to be grateful for every family you have, be it birth related, adopted, or connected through your soul.

Acknowledgments

I would like to acknowledge all the wonderful and loving people in my life. Without their support and compassion, I would not be the person I am today and this book would have never been.

My first and very special thanks is to my parents, my late father Karl Heinz and my wonderful, loving, and caring mother Christiane. I owe my parents the best upbringing a child can have and the love only true parents can give. The next thanks goes to my wonderful brother Christopher, who is the most generous person I have ever met. I feel blessed to have him as my brother and I know that he will always be there for me as I hope he knows I will be for him.

My next thanks is to my birth parents. My birth mother Edda, who did what she knew was the best for me even though it meant for her to lose a child. I thank her husband Karl, who supported his wife in meeting me even though he was afraid it would disrupt his own family relations. To my birth father Ottie, who embraces the presence and made me feel at home from the first time we ever met. I especially thank him and his wife Irene to help me publish this book.

I also like to say thanks to my new sisters Amelie, Sophie and Christine, who greeted me with curiosity into their family, even if sometimes our differences in character make our relationship somewhat difficult. I like to thank my brothers Monte, Matthew and Chad and my little sister Samantha, who did not think at all that is was strange to call me their new sister and who have the gift to accept me as the person I am.

In addition, I would like to thank all my wonderful friends in Germany and the US, like Astrid, Anne, Andrea, Bärbel, Gülay, Carole, Jen, Jenny, Mark and Debbie, Jackie, and Ellen, just to name a few, and my dear cousins Andrea and Thomas, who believed in me and love me unconditionally. What a gift, to have such friends. I also like to thank my friend Bill Livick, editor of the *Oregon Observer*, for providing the picture of me.

I especially thank my dearest friends Connie and Heike, who have generously and critically read my first drafts, their endless comments and ideas to make this book what it is today, and who always supported me emotionally and professionally. To Emilee Mead and Joyce Gilmour, my two awesome editors who have helped me perfect my ideas into a readable for appropriate for a book to be published. Especially Joyce Gilmour, who herself is an adoptive Mom, and my daughters most wonderful 3rd Grade teacher, has spend her valuable free time to edit my book twice to make it what it is today.

And last, but not least, I want to thank my wonderful and loving husband Ross, for always supporting me and my new adventures and our two wonderful children, who grow up in a world where you can never have enough loving family members. Carmen and Sean have early on accepted that there was a seemingly endless amount of aunts and uncles and more grandparents than most children have.

Without all those people, my book would have most likely just been an idea which never materialized. It was up to them to make it happen.

Julia Meyers

Coffee and Cake

– An Adoptee –
in Search of Her Past

CHAPTER 1
Waking Up

I awoke with a sudden jolt, knowing the time had come. I had to write her a letter. I had to tell her I was fine, and above all I had to tell her that, not only did I accept her decision, I was grateful for what she had done twenty-eight years earlier. This person that I knew I had to contact was my birth mother. Almost thirty years earlier I was born to a German mother and an American soldier, a man who disappeared without a trace shortly after I was conceived. My mother, with little income or support, wanted me to have a good home with both a mother and a father. After a difficult struggle, she placed me for adoption. My birth mother was not told the names of my adoptive parents, nor where I was moved. My birth certificate, with her name and address, was the only item I had that connected me to her.

I sometimes wondered if Edda, my birth mother, looked like me at all. I am not a particularly tall person at 5 feet 4 inches, but I always liked my height. I never really wanted to be taller. Did I get that height from her? I wondered if Edda was blond too, if her hair was straight like mine, or curly like my hair was when I was a little child.

I do not remember what made me come to the decision to write a letter that memorable day, far from my home in Germany. Was it a dream? Perhaps. Even though it was mid-January in the Sonoran Desert of Tucson, Arizona, it was unseasonably hot. I arrived there a week prior, my sleep cycle had yet to adjust to the nine-hour time difference. I would wake up at 4:00 or 5:00 a.m., unable to fall asleep again. I would make myself a cup of coffee and have a blueberry bagel with strawberry cream cheese, a new delight I had just discovered, since we do not have bagels in Germany. I would then bike to the university where I was working as an intern, analyzing ceramics in an archaeology laboratory.

That day, I biked home about 3:00 p.m., which still felt like midnight to me, and I laid down for a nap. I was planning to sleep just a little while, and later go out with my roommate, Patrick, and his friends. I met Patrick four years earlier, on my first excavation in the U.S., and we had stayed friends over the years. When I came this year for a four-month internship at the archaeology laboratory of the university, he offered me the empty bedroom in his little rented house. It was a sure thing. Patrick is a kind and generous person, and I was sure to be safe with him. He is tall and strong, and I think he is one of the smartest people I have ever met. He is very literate, but unlike me, he can remember everything he has ever read. Patrick was in graduate school at the University of Arizona and I took a Hopi Language class with him. We were good roommates, and Patrick was so kind to take me along to visit his friends in the evenings. He had a new girlfriend, Hilary, who lived as a roommate in a house that belonged to Patrick's friend Ross. I remember the first time Patrick took me to their house. He told me how wonderful Ross was, and that he owned his house! I think for Patrick this was a sign of maturity and self-determination.

I will never forget seeing Ross the first time. We went to the house, and Hilary opened the door. She seemed nice, had dark brown curly hair, and a big smile. Then they brought me to this big, dark, smelly back room of the house, where a guy with long, light-brown hair was playing a black guitar and singing. I was told that this was Ross. He sat on a bar stool and played his guitar, not really noticing anything around him, including me. He barely acknowledged me, but since Patrick and Hilary went off, I stayed and listened. Ross had an amazing voice and was a very gifted guitar player. I was not sure what to think of him, though. I was glad when Patrick and Hilary came back. Over the weeks, all four of us became friends, and we used to watch *Friends* and *Seinfeld* on TV together, or study in a coffee shop. Ross's dog, Xenon, (named after the chemical element) took a liking to me, and every time I came over to visit, that big 70-pound Greyhound mix with the big dark eyes would sit on my lap!

But let me go back to that special day in mid-January. When I woke up that day, the only thing I could think of was Edda, and the decision that had found its way into my thoughts and into my soul: a decision that had now irreversibly anchored itself into my mind. The only thing I knew about my birth mother, other than her name, was that she had a difficult time deciding on the adoption, and that afterwards, she had contacted the adoption agency several times to inquire about my well-being.

Why now? All my life I had known I was adopted. Certainly I wondered about my birth mother, if I had siblings, what they looked like, just generally who these people were. But I never really had the urge to find out. In fact, I had no reason to find out. I had wonderful parents, a great brother, a nice home, and I grew up in a beautiful small Rhineland community in central Germany. My parents always told us that my brother was adopted too, and that real parents are not those who conceive and give birth to you, but those who raise you. I had no reason to question this.

When I say that I knew all of my life that I was adopted, I mean that literally. The adoption agency officer advised my parents to make the fact that we are adopted as normal as possible, by telling us from early childhood on. So, while other mothers said to their babies, "You are so cute my baby," our mother would say, "You are so cute, and I am so thankful for your birth mothers' decisions to grant us such a wonderful gift." That is the best advice I have ever heard. I know many people who are adopted, including my own brother Christopher and my cousin, Andrea. Unfortunately, when one hears about adoptions that were kept secret, they almost always end in disaster. The basic trust between parent and child is broken once the child, often by accident, finds out he or she was adopted. My brother and I just always knew. It was part of who we were. And sometimes, it is actually easier to deal with your family when you can say, "Thank goodness, we are not blood-related!" And yet, we would sometimes make a game of finding similarities between us, such as size, clothing preference, hair color, or other characteristics. We were especially delighted when an unsuspecting neighbor told us we looked similar to our parents.

Had anything substantial changed to precipitate this sudden decision to contact my mother? No, not really. Maybe, instead, I was simply growing up. I had finished high school, ended my first teenage "love," worked at a bank, started a master's program in anthropology at the Johann Wolfgang Goethe University in Frankfurt, Germany, been on an archaeological excavation in Winslow, Arizona, followed my first real big love to Argentina, lived there for a while, finished my master's degree in Germany, learned that love must be two-sided to work, and ended up back in Arizona as an intern at the Arizona State Museum.

In Tucson, I thought occasionally about how to write the letter to Edda, but I could not decide what to write. When I woke up that fateful day, I knew I had made the decision, although I did not know how to go about it. First, other than my birth certificate that had her name and address, I had no idea where she might be. Secondly, what would I say? So, I sat down at my battered, small, gray metal desk in my little house. I took out my beautiful black ink pen and a piece of paper and ... did not know how to begin. How do you address a mother you have never known? Was this even the right thing to do? What if her family did not know about me, and through this letter found out? What if it created trouble for Edda? I did not even want to think about that. What a big responsibility it was to write this letter. What a huge decision. What if she did not want her family to know about me? What if Edda did not want to hear from me?

CHAPTER 2

The Letter

I came back to Germany in April of that same year, 1996, and after two weeks of vacation, started working in the "Königspfalz." I was the field director for a wonderful project in one of Charlemagne's 114 castles[1]. The castle where I worked, "Königspfalz Ingelheim," is a gorgeous site and the staff is fantastic. That particular site is located in Ingelheim, a neighbor to my hometown, also located on the picturesque Rhine River. The throne room is still partially standing, with walls as high as three stories. The outer, defensive walls, later added to the castle by Otto I, are some three meters thick. Some still exhibit the walkway on their upper part, with the narrow openings for shooting arrows still in place. The foundation of the church, located within the premises of the site, is also from the time of Charlemagne, and it is said that he spent several Easter ceremonies at this particular site.

My boss and I got along famously. Working for him was great, all I had to do was be outside, no matter if there was sun, rain, or snow, sit in the dirt, and organize the excavation. I managed up to thirty people, working in up to four different places throughout the site. There were high school and university students, long-term unemployed workers sent from the city, and professional archaeologists. I like people, and I love excavating. I did not like to present the results at archaeological meetings or to the city. Instead, I liked to take the photo-

[1]Charlemagne (A.D. 742-814) was king of the Franks from A.D. 768-814, and emperor of the Holy Roman Empire from A.D. 800-814. He is one of Europe's most well-known and important historical leaders. He unified an enormous empire, including countries known today as France, Germany, Belgium, Netherlands, and northern Italy. Charlemagne was known as a mobile king and emperor, who traveled to various regions of his empire to instill his power through his presence.

graphs, make the drawings, organize the crews, make sure my high school students, and everyone else, were kept busy and happy. I think that the several surprise parties given for me show that I was a good boss. It was the best job I ever had.

I was living with my parents and enjoying being pampered once more. My parents are fourteen years apart in age. My father was in the Second World War, forced to join at the age of seventeen, and was captured by American soldiers. He always told us that this had saved his life. His growth, though, had stagnated through this event, and because of the delay through the war he could not go to college. Instead he learned to be a business administrator at a big pharmaceutical company, and was sent to South America to establish business connections. When he came home, he met my twenty-three-year old mother at the tennis court. My father was always very active and looked much younger than he was. His skin was always brown, and with his black hair and his knowledge in the Spanish language he could have easily been taken for a man of Latino descent. When I moved back home, my father was experiencing some serious health issues, and resulting operations causing his former strength to fade.

My mother is a kind and loving person. However, her inability to not say what is on her mind could bring her into some serious trouble. I remember as a school-age child my mother would become furious if she thought a teacher was mistreating my brother or me. She would march off to school and give that teacher a piece of her mind.

It was nice to be close to my parents, and to my brother. My brother Christopher is three years younger than me, and we get along famously. I am not lying, but I have to admit, when we were younger, that was not always the case. As many older sisters are probably able to report, having a younger sibling, who constantly wants to do the same thing you do, can be a pain in the butt. Christopher was a very petite little boy, but as I got older, he outgrew me by about one foot! I am now his 'little sister' and he can be quite protective of me.

I also enjoyed being close to my childhood friends. Although most of them were still at universities or had started their careers, most came home on the weekends, and we always found ways to enjoy that time together. There is no lack of festivals, cozy bars, or places to have an outdoor barbeque.

One evening, while my parents, brother, and I were all sitting in the living room enjoying the warmth of the fire from our fireplace and enjoying a peaceful cup of coffee and homemade cake, I told them about my plans to write Edda. My parents were not surprised, and they fully supported my decision. This was a great relief to me, because I did not want to do anything to upset my parents, and having their understanding meant a lot to me. They are my parents and I love them very much. Most of all, I did not want to do anything to hurt them in any way.

Then came the next step of finding my birth mother's address and new name. My first inquiry was to the township where my mother's address had been listed at the time of my birth. Unexpectedly, I received an answer within a week, telling me her married name and a new address. Just as fast as I received an answer from that first township, information came from the second. This time I received not only her next address, but her current address. I realized she moved about ten times during the last thirty years! It was all so fast and so unexpected that for a few weeks I could not work on the letter at all!

During this time, my good friend Chris arrived from Tucson. Chris and I met in Tucson during the four months I was there, and we instantly became friends. She was a petite person, with skin so white it almost looked like porcelain, and beautiful, black, long, thick hair. I love long hair, but mine is thin and does not seem to want to grow beyond a certain length. There was something about Chris that fascinated me, and I could not help but be drawn to her from the first time I met her at the laboratory. She shared my love for coffee, and we would take coffee breaks almost daily. I was grateful to have another friend, and enjoyed her company enormously. Chris had never left the U.S. and I asked my boss if she could come along as a paid crewmember to help me excavate for three months.

Not wanting to bother my parents, and also wanting to have some fun without parental supervision (did you realize that parents always treat you like a small child no matter how old you get?), Chris and I moved to a small apartment close to the site, which was provided by the excavation project. That was fun. It had almost no furniture, was difficult to heat, and all in all, it was very sparse. We slept on mattresses on the floor and had a minimum of furniture to get along. But what a great place to have parties!

My students absolutely loved giving me beer, so they would often come by unexpectedly after work, bringing some good German beer. Yes, I am German, but for some reason, I just cannot drink. After only a quarter glass of beer, I start feeling dizzy. This is no fun for me at all; but apparently it is for others. No, I do not behave badly (unless you call laughing without being able to stop badly), I just have a very difficult time concentrating or keeping my balance. My very good friend and soul mate, Connie, who I met during one of my first classes at the Goethe University in Frankfurt, always joked that the intolerance for alcohol might stem from my possible Native American ancestry. After all, my birth father was American.

Since I was a child I wanted to live in America. Native Americans always aroused my interest, and I was obsessed with learning more about different ethnic groups. As a child, I dressed up as an "Indian" for Carnival. I even had a little fort, "Fort Laramie," where the Indians always won the battles. I think many Germans are obsessed with Native Americans. Part of this obsession can be credited to the well-known East German author Karl May, an ex-con, who started writing adventure books while in jail for petty crimes. Probably the best-known books of Karl May include a trilogy centered on a fictional Mescalero Apache chief *Winnetou*, who had the noblest of all human spirits. Winnetou's character is complemented by Old Shatterhand, a German friend, who becomes his blood brother in the first book. In the final part of the trilogy, Winnetou sacrifices his life for his brother. This sacrifice finally brings peace to the white settlers and the Apaches. Karl May, who did not actually see "real Indians" until much later in his life, created the legacy of the noble Indian in Europe. This legacy spread the seed for many generations of Germans, especially students, me included, to collect signatures for American Indian Movement members in support of their fight to assure Native Americans' rights. Hobby groups all over Germany recreate Native American life-styles, living them on the weekends. They choose their favorite tribe, and re-create their houses, their clothing, and even their dances. I participated in one of these weekend gatherings, including a sweat lodge ceremony, and it was quite nice. Although it was a little strange to pretend to be someone else, I liked the fact that a group of people would live outside in beautiful teepees, some families of up to three generations in one tent, getting away from TV and Internet, just enjoying nature and each other.

My personal obsession with America and Native Americans was nourished when I was sixteen-years-old and my mother told me nonchalantly that my birth father an American soldier! This was new to me, and I was ecstatic! Maybe that explains why I had an odd eye shape that people sometimes asked me about. Maybe I was part Native American! One should never give up dreaming!

While Chris and I were living in our little apartment, I finally made some progress on the letter to Edda. The most difficult part was how to begin. How do you address a mother you have never known? Should I write "Dear Mother," or simply "Dear Edda?" The old question of whether this was the right thing to do came up again. I knew that this was a big responsibility. If I wrote this letter there would be no return. I would have to face the results of my actions. I decided that, given what I knew about Edda, she must want to know about me. My parents told me everything the adoption agency had conveyed to them. My birth mother, who was the same age as my mother, had been engaged to an American soldier. They had met at a dance, and dated for a few months. Then, he suddenly disappeared, and when Edda realized he was gone for good, she decided she wanted me to have a stable environment with a father and a mother, so she considered adoption. She moved to her sister's house so no one at home would know she was pregnant. The adoption was a very difficult decision for Edda. During the first two months of my life, which, according to the law, I spent in an orphanage, she changed her mind about the adoption several times. So, my parents were somewhat unprepared, but very relieved, when they received a call from the agency saying they could pick me up. Edda wrote several letters to the adoption agency after I was adopted, asking about my development and well-being. The agency would tell my parents, and my mother would write back to the agency. She never wrote directly to my birth mother, who did not know them or even their names. I remember going to the agency with my mother and talking to "our" social worker. I liked it there because they had fun toys. When I was about eight years old, our social worker passed away, and we never went there again. Also, my parents were not asked for information about me after that.

As for Edda's "imaginary" family, they were not as imaginary as you may think. Through those letters, my parents learned that she married a year after I was born and had at least one other child, about three years younger than me. I did not learn this, however, until after I told my parents about my intent to write. I had siblings! But who knew how many? What did they look like? What did they do? Were they healthy, happy, married? Almost more than meeting my birth parents, having siblings was an exciting prospective. All my life I wanted lots of siblings. Maybe, my wish would now be granted. I looked at the empty page again, the page on which I was trying to write my letter. What I needed was a cup of coffee to calm me down. I walked into the kitchen, which also served as a living, dining, and study room, and started making coffee. It would be several more weeks before I finally finished the letter, which, reading it years later, seems immature and shaky.

Gau-Algesheim, October 14, 1996

Dear Edda,

I am not quite sure how to begin this letter, even though I feel that I know exactly what I want to write. I am certain, you are wondering why I am writing you at this time and I will try to explain it to you the best I can.

Of course, as a child, I sometimes wondered who you were. But it was mere curiosity and I neither wanted to hurt my parents, nor tear open wounds which might have healed by now. My brother, who is three years younger than me, and I, always knew that we were adopted. It seemed normal and natural to us and we would have never doubted who our true parents were. I can even remember vividly how we visited my brother at the orphanage and how we later picked him up. For the longest time I believed that children come from an orphanage.

But now back to the reason of my letter. I have traveled a lot all over the world and have lived in the United States as well as in the Andes of Argentina. I have met many different kinds of people and have learned many important things in life, especially while living a rather simple life in the Andes. I have learned that there are more important things than money and wealth in one's life; and one of those things is to say "thank you" or to tell someone you love them. Those are sometimes difficult things to say and many times they go unsaid. But why? Life is too short and people should tell each other much more frequently how they feel about each other.

I have always thought very highly of you and I felt very sad for you. I have been raised very lovingly and protected and have always been very happy with my life. Of course, I had always wanted to know why I had been adopted and my parents told me willingly everything they knew. Never have they said anything bad or negative about you. That had been very important to me. My parents always told me that I am really similar to you and that you had suffered for having given me up for adoption. That is why suddenly I had the urge to write to you.

I wanted to say thanks through this letter, thanks for my life - I am a pretty strong advocate against abortion - and thanks for having taken the burden of giving me to parents, and with that giving me the life I am able to live right now. And thanks that you did not just push me away without any emotion or love as it had been the case of my brother's birth mother.

I love my life and that is why I thought I would tell you a little about myself. My original plan was to tell you all this after I got married, but since this might take a little longer than I had anticipated, I decided to not wait any longer. I love children very much and sometimes write children's stories. Writing has a special meaning to me since I am dyslexic and to be able to write means the world to me. Already early in life I loved to travel. I started when I was just two years old, taking the two-hour bus by myself to visit my grandparents; now I am traveling back and forth from Argentina, USA, and Germany. I am an archaeologist and this is part of what I do.

My life was not always like this though. When I was fifteen I had my first boyfriend. He was a painter and we wanted to get married, so when I finished high school, I started an apprenticeship at the bank to have steady work and an income. But that is when I suddenly had a realization. That could not be my life! I wanted to go to the university and travel. My boyfriend and I separated peacefully and today he lives with his wife and children close to my parents' house and we see each other from time to time. Then I began to study anthropology and to travel. It was like a dream! I enjoyed every day of being a student and took every class I could find about North or South America. I also studied Spanish.

One of my aunts lives in California and I visited her the first time when I was sixteen years old. Being a student I used my summer vacation to travel for three months crisscross through the United States. In 1992, I went for an archaeological excavation to Arizona. This is when my life once again changed dramatically. I regularly went back to participate in the excavation and I also met a wonder-

ful man who took me to Argentina. He is an archaeologist, too, and together we lived in a small beautiful Andean village. It was like a paradise to me. I lived there altogether for about sixteen months, sometimes without electricity or running water. I had eight dogs and a sheep. Some of the natives called me San Roque, the saint of the animals. Unfortunately, Axel and I separated last December, because our visions about the future differed too much.

In the meantime I finished my Masters Thesis about "Wall Paintings of the Anasazi" and am now preparing for my PhD dissertation. I applied for the PhD program at the University of Arizona, and I will return to Arizona in January. At the moment, I am a field director of a medieval excavation at one of Charlemagne castles in Germany. It is located in Ingelheim, close to where I grew up. I love to work outside and it gives me the opportunity to be close to my parents, since my father has been very sick. I am living with my two American friends, also archaeologists, in a small apartment close to the site. It is not very big but we have a lot of fun.

Well, this is a short version of my life. I hope that this letter brings you a little bit of happiness and that I did not hurt you in any way by contacting you. I have wanted to write this letter for a long time.

With love,
Julia

If you think I went right out and sent the letter, you would be mistaken. That took some time, including several trips to the post office, just to turn away again. One day though, after work, I took the letter to the yellow mailbox next to our excavation office. In Germany, public mailboxes are yellow, and they are spread throughout town, because we do not use our own mailboxes to send letters, as is common custom in the US. It was September of 1996, a sunny day with a nice chill in the air that announced fall, and turned the trees into the most beautiful colors imaginable. I stood there, next to the bright yellow box, literally shaking, not from the chilly air, but from anxiety. What am I doing? Was this the right decision? What if she was not the way I imagined her? What if she did not want to hear from me? How had I imagined her? I was not sure. I was told that phenotypically she was similar to me, so I thought blond and not very tall. More importantly, how did I imagine her character? All the information I had about my birth mother came from my parents. According to that vague information, I envisioned her as kind, sensitive, and of course, overjoyed to see me. But what if she was not? What if she had wanted to forget her past, and me? I finally threw the letter into the mailbox. Then I waited. Right there. I could not leave. I actually considered waiting for the mailman to ask him for the letter back. Finally, I decided to leave. My stomach started aching, and I felt like throwing up. I could not sleep that first night.

But then nothing happened. Nothing happened for six long weeks. During the first couple of weeks I was very nervous, running to the mailbox everyday, expecting a reply. After a while I gave up and found a sort of peace in not getting an answer. Maybe it was better that way. Who knows what would have happened if she had replied? Just as I started to relax, a letter arrived. I was very nervous, which is a huge understatement. I carried the unopened letter with me the entire day. I did not want to read it with anyone else around. I knew I would be very emotional, and I did not want anybody to see me like that. Finally, I went into my boss's office after everyone had gone home for the night. I sat in his big office chair and stared at the letter. What would it say? Would she want to see me? Would she tell me not to contact her again? Finally, I opened it.

The letter was short, polite, and very carefully written. Edda wanted to know if I was sure that she was the one for which I was looking. When exactly was my birthday and was I maybe born under a different name? I could not believe what I had just read, and I immediately realized my mistake. I was too surprised to cry. Yes, she was the right woman, and yes, how could I have forgotten, I was born with a different name; the name she had given me at birth. Of course, she could not know my parents changed my first name, and she had never known my new last name! This poor woman! From her letter, I could tell how much she wanted it to be me and how she was trying not to be too enthusiastic about my letter in case it might not be me. The letters she received from the adoption agency had probably not used my new name to keep my family's identity safe. I immediately called my parents from the little office. They were relieved she finally answered, because their main concern was that I not be hurt by this experience. The same night, I wrote Edda a second letter. This time, the writing went much faster. In fact, I wrote the letter without any hesitation. I even sent the letter the next day, this time without the stomachache. And ... I only had to wait two days for an answer.

Edda's second letter was much more emotional, and for me, stirring. I cried so much reading how she held me when I was born, knowing it would be the last time she would see me. This poor woman...how much pain must she have endured all those years? She told me she had three more daughters, but not a day went by that she did not think about me. When she gave birth to her fourth child, under the influence of narcotics, she said my name. Her husband, unaware that this was my name, thought she wanted that to be the name of his daughter, and he gave her my name! She always thought she was the only mother in the world with two daughters, both born in January, with exactly the same name: Christine. As I suspected, the adoption agency never told her my parents had changed my name.

Edda wrote that, when she was pregnant with me, she felt great, as if nothing could come between us since I was safe inside of her. However, giving birth to me was traumatic, not physically, but mentally, because she knew that she had lost me. Edda and her husband met a year after I was born, and they married the following year. Although her husband knew about me, their daughters did not. She told me she wanted to tell them eventually; she also expressed the desire to meet me. Edda lived in northern Germany, so we had to find a time and place that was good for both of us. Edda's late parents had lived in a town close to my hometown and were buried there. She decided to combine a visit to their graves with our meeting. In her third letter, she proposed to meet Monday, December 2 of 1996, at 1:21 p.m., when she would arrive by train to this little town. That would be a day I would never, ever forget, but unfortunately, for two reasons.

CHAPTER 3

Roller Coaster

It was cold that morning of December 2. This day would be imprinted in my mind by two seemingly unrelated events, which would, through their power of synchronicity, ultimately be inseparable. I know this does not make sense at this moment, but the notion of ying and yang would become meaningful for the first time in my life.

I woke up early that day, and was nervous and excited at the same time. What would happen? Today I would meet Edda, my birth mother, for the very first time. Would I recognize her? After all, I had never seen a picture of her. What would I say? Would we cry? Would she like me? Question after question, none of which I could answer. This day would almost certainly change my life forever; I just did not know yet in what fundamental ways. I even briefly considered not going to meet her at all, to just pretend I had never written the letter. But it had been my choice, my decision, and now I had to face the consequences. Oh yes, I wanted to meet her, to get to know her. But at the same time, I was afraid. This is different than meeting just anybody; this meeting had the potential to change my life forever. Not that I would really change, but my feelings, the image I had of myself, would be altered. I would meet the woman who had given birth to me, the woman who decided my life was more important than hers, and that I should have a family, even if it meant she would never see me again, her own flesh and blood.

I admired my parents. They did not seem nervous at all. They knew I was not meeting her to find a new family; they knew my loyalty was to them. When they got married, my parents had plans for a big family. But things went differently. They were unable to get pregnant, and after four years of trying and many doctor visits, they finally realized that if they wanted to have children, they needed to adopt them. At that time, parents had to be a certain age to legally adopt children. My mother, at twenty-eight years of age, was considered too young; however, my father, being fourteen years older than my mother, was the right age. After a lot of consulting, they were allowed to foster, and later adopt, a child. The first child they were offered was a little boy who was already born. He had gypsy ancestry – a word commonly used in Germany to describe people of Sinti or Roma descent, who used to earn their living by traveling through the country selling handcrafted goods. But they were afraid he would have the "traveling blood," and would want to leave home early to travel the world. Boy, were they wrong in adopting me! My poor parents. If there is something like a "gypsy blood," I definitely have it. I was the next child presented to my parents. I was not born yet, so my gender was not known. My parents agreed to adopt, though, regardless of gender. Edda moved to her sister's to finish her pregnancy and give birth anonymously.

I was born January 29, 1968, and placed into an orphanage, according to a law that has since been changed. Babies who were supposed to be adopted were put into an orphanage for the first three months of their lives, to give birth parents time to rethink their decision. However, during this time, the birth parents, nor the potential parents, were allowed to visit the baby. This was a horrendous practice by today's standard. My birth mother did find a compassionate nurse who would occasionally let her hold me. My mother, who had worked in the hospital where the orphanage was located, also found a way to visit me from time to time. When those two leaks in the security system were discovered, I was relocated. I was two months old at that time. That was when Edda told the adoption agency she wanted me to be adopted. She wanted me to be with my parents immediately. My parents, who had not known if they would definitely be able to have me or not, received the long-awaited call. They could pick me up the following day! My mother called my father at work, and then ran to town to buy the most essential baby attire. According to the law, I had to be a foster child for one year, after which time my parents could adopt me. This old rule, which provided the adoption agency with the option to take their child back if they saw any signs of neglect or abuse in the adopting family, is no longer in use.

And then, twenty-eight years later, I was about to meet my birth mother. After a very light breakfast – I could barely get anything down – and a shower, I was ready. But I still had a few hours until I had to leave. It was difficult to concentrate or do anything. I sat in my room meditating about what lay ahead. When it was lunchtime, and though I had barely eaten breakfast, I could not get anything down. I was too nervous. Finally, it was time for me to leave. I took my parents' car, a small red Mazda 363 sports version. Although I knew the way, I was terrified I would not find the town or the train station. I arrived much too early, of course. I stood there, dressed in my black wool coat with a bright red Poncho Salteño over my shoulders. I bought this poncho in Argentina and loved its color. I wore it all the time, and it looked great over my black coat, especially because the poncho had two black vertical stripes on one side, over the shoulder. I told Edda on the phone that I would wear this poncho, so she could recognize me.

I checked the train schedule and went to the appropriate platform. It was quite cold, but I was sweating. I had to wait about fifteen minutes. Then the signal turned green and I could see the train slowly coming into the station. I was so nervous. The train arrived at the station, and I tried to look through the passing doors to see her. A woman was standing behind one of the doors. Then the train came to a halt, the door opened, and a woman, who could only be Edda, stepped down the two steps onto the platform. Because no one else exited the train, I knew it had to be her. I walked toward this fifty-six-year-old woman with grey, curly hair, trying to smile and trying not to cry. It was somewhat awkward, but somehow, we managed to hug each other. Almost thirty years of wondering, regretting, feeling guilty, feeling a loss, and being endlessly grateful were poured into this first, self-conscious, yet wonderful hug. Then, we both cried. We quickly tried to pull ourselves together. After all, we had not really met yet – if you do not consider the birthing room at the hospital – and did not want the other to feel uneasy or embarrassed. Edda and I were almost exactly the same height, except I was about one inch taller. I also found some similarities in our eyes, but other than that it was really hard to tell on the first impression. Very importantly though, she seemed to be a very kind and loving person, and that was something for which I could not have wished.

We went to the cemetery first. Edda showed me the grave of her parents. She was sincerely sad that I could never meet them. They did not know about me, but somehow, they must have felt it. Edda told me that when I finally left the orphanage at two and a half months of age, she took the train to see her parents. Although she had not told them she was coming, her father was waiting for her at the train station! Her parents never asked her what happened, but they welcomed her quite warmly. Being the youngest child, Edda has two older siblings and her parents were somewhat older when she was born.

Edda and I decided to go to a small restaurant to eat something light, and then go for a walk along the picturesque Nahe River. Edda brought several family photo albums. I could not believe it when I saw her childhood pictures. She could have been my twin, except she had curly brown hair and I have blond, mostly straight hair. My half-sisters, three, five, and seven years younger than me, look more like their father. As little girls, however, we looked a lot alike. For me, that was the strangest thing of all. All my life, I thought of myself as unique. I never met anyone who looked like me, let alone four people. Edda's sister also looks very similar to me. This was very difficult for my self-esteem. It was interesting and confusing, at the same time, to learn so much about my past. I fought very hard to become who I am, and now there were people, more than one, who apparently not only looked like me, but also had behavioral characteristics similar to mine. Who was I then, just an image, a genetic duplicate of somebody else?

Edda told me her husband knew about me, and when they married, he said he would have married her even if she had a child. Although this was meant very generously, it intensified Edda's feelings of guilt about and for me. Not knowing if I was fine, that I did indeed have a good life, caring parents, and happiness, was a burning pain in her heart. Edda told me that for almost a year now – coinciding with the time I had decided to contact her – she and her husband had waited for a sign from me. Edda watched local television more closely to see if she would recognize me, in case I was a public person, and her husband even dreamed about my reappearance. He was not surprised to see my letter; however, he did have some objections. He was concerned about Edda's reputation and the well-being of his three daughters. I understood his doubts as this is his family, and he needs to protect them from harm.

Although I was extremely curious, I thought that the first meeting was not the appropriate time to ask about my birth father. However, Edda told me a little bit about him. She said he had been an eighteen-year-old American soldier, and they had been engaged. She told me that, when she first told him she was pregnant, he seemed excited and he fantasized about having a boy. But then, suddenly, he disappeared and she never heard from him again. She tried everything to keep me, including advertisements in the newspaper with the words, "Who will still take me?" She was desperate, trying to keep us together. She received over 150 responding letters mainly from creepy people and one medical doctor trying to convince her to abort me. Finally, she decided to give me up for adoption.

I had made a small photo album for Edda as a present, with pictures of my life until our meeting, including pictures of me as a baby, a toddler, my first day at school, growing up, my first boyfriend, and me at an excavation. I also included a picture of my brother and my parents. I wanted her to have some visual idea of what my life had been like. I think that, while this meant a lot to Edda, it also made her sad because she had not been there for these parts of my life. I assured her that from now on, she would be part of my life and would be able to participate.

Edda had a present for me: an old red-colored mechanical alarm clock. Why that, you might ask. Well, let me tell you the story Edda told me that day: this was her alarm clock when she was pregnant with me. During the pregnancy, the alarm clock suddenly started malfunctioning. Every evening at exactly 6:35 p.m. the alarm clock would stop working and get stuck. In the morning, though, at 6:35 a.m. it would continue unhindered. Edda took the alarm clock to a repair shop, to no result. I was born at exactly 6:35 p.m. The alarm clock never stuck again, until it finally just stopped working years later. Edda kept the alarm clock for me in case I ever returned.

Finally, it was time for us to part. We promised to keep in contact from now on, and to write each other. I was leaving for Tucson again in three weeks, and we both wanted to get to know each other better. I had prepared myself for this meeting for almost a year and now it was over. I had lots of things about which to think. I am the kind of person who needs time to consider everything and who needs to sleep over events first, before I can comprehend everything. I am a scientist after all, and I need to look at everything for a long time from various angles. But what happened next was completely unexpected, and I do not think one can ever be prepared for such an event.

When I arrived home that night, I was excited and exhausted, and I wanted to tell my parents all about it. For some reason though, I decided to read my e-mails first, probably to calm down. My parents were curious, but knowing me, and my habit of having to digest new events before talking about them, did not push me to tell them about Edda? Edda and my meeting, and did not mind that I first looked at my e-mails. The first e-mail was from my friend Jill, who I had met in Tucson and who had spent three weeks excavating with me in Germany. Jill had been Chris's friend back in Tucson, and when she heard that Chris was coming with me to Germany, Jill asked if she could join us for three weeks. I agreed, although I had only met Jill briefly, in Tucson. The three weeks with all three of us together was fun, and I became quite fond of Jill; like Chris she was some years younger than me. Jill had not only become friends with me, she also become friends with my brother. All four of us had a great time together, and the three weeks passed like the wind. At the end of those three weeks, I took her to the train station so she could go to the Frankfurt airport to fly to Romania. She had a boyfriend there that she met in Tucson. Without telling her parents, she was planning to marry him in Romania so they could go to the U.S. together. Well, at least that was what she had planned to do when she first arrived in Germany. Then, several events started to change her mind, and she was not sure if she really wanted to marry him. Actually, she knew she did not want to marry him. However, she wanted to tell him in person, because they dated for quite a while in Tucson.

Several people in Germany told her not to go. Romania did not seem like a very safe country for a twenty-year old girl at that time. We advised her to just call him and not to go all the way to Romania to see him. Many people told her that, but she wanted to go. She felt it was her duty to tell him the bad news in person. When I last saw her at the train station in Ingelheim, she was nervously playing with a Rubik's Cube.

Her e-mail was written in German, which was strange, since she did not speak German very well and had never spoken to me in German before. The content of the e-mail was confusing, and because of the bad German I did not completely understand her. It almost seemed as if she was afraid to write in English. My interpretation of the e-mail was that she initially decided to get married, but then suddenly, possibly at the wedding, decided not to go through with it. She wrote that she was going to fly home the next day, and was looking forward to seeing me in Tucson again when I returned. At the end of the letter, there was a small English note for Christopher, that she was looking forward to seeing my brother when he would come to visit Tucson in February.

The second e-mail was from a good friend in Tucson. What I read froze the blood in my veins. For a moment I could not breathe. The world stopped turning. The sentence I read was: "Have you heard that Jill is dead? There was some sort of an accident and they are both dead." Thinking of this still makes my stomach turn, and my heart stop. At first, I refused to acknowledge this horrible fact. It was impossible. I had just read Jill's e-mail; she could not be dead! I checked the time on the two e-mails. It was almost impossible to decipher the real times of the two e-mails, because of the time differences among the three countries. Finally, all I knew was that there had been a few hours difference between the first and the second e-mail, and that she most likely died immediately after she wrote the e-mail to me. I kept telling myself she could not be dead. Frantic, I called her parents in Tucson. It was about 5:00 a.m. in Tucson, but her father picked up the phone immediately. It was true, Jill and her ex-boyfriend were dead. But it was not an accident. He had killed her, beaten her to death and then hung himself!

I think I cried for three weeks straight. I still cry when I think about her: it is so painful. In German there is a saying that happiness and pain are right next to each other, and it was the first time I understood the meaning of this. A new mother and a horrible death forever linked in my mind. I could never again separate these two events from each other. No matter how many years followed, and how often Edda wrote excitedly about how long we have known each other, I would think about Jill and the pain of her death. It reminds me that there is no joy without suffering, no happiness without sadness, no ying without yang. A mother gained a child that day, while another mother lost one. And somehow I, even though those events were separated by an ocean, had connected them in a way I could not comprehend.

The next few weeks passed in a fog. I was on a roller coaster of emotions. I actually do not remember any details about that time, until I left for Tucson, three weeks later. I was able to get over Jill's death. I cried so much that it seems, in the end, my tears dried up; I was empty, without any feelings. To lose someone through a senseless, violent crime is almost impossible to comprehend. In the meantime, Edda wrote a letter, which arrived just two days after we had met. Understandably, she wanted to know if she was how I had imagined her, or if I was disappointed. She was so afraid I might not like her. It was difficult to concentrate on her now, to consider the feelings of a woman who had regained her lost child, while I had lost a friend in the most incomprehensible way possible. What could or should I write her? What should I tell her? It felt so little, like writing to Edda or dealing with anything. I had to learn that life was going on around me, and I was part of it.

CHAPTER 4

Back to Tucson

The second of January 1997, exactly a month after I had met Edda and Jill had been killed, I flew back to Tucson. My plan was to work at the Homol'ovi Laboratory again, and maybe take one class at the university. I also decided to officially apply at the University of Arizona for the Ph.D. program in archaeology. Although I had sworn to never go through all the trouble of getting a Ph.D., it seemed the most logical decision. I wanted to study in Arizona and I wanted to become an archaeologist, and I already had a Masters Degree. And to top it off, since my first visit and excavation in 1992, the beauty of the desert captured me and its magic had invaded my soul. Archaeology became the dream of my life.

This whole life-changing event began in 1991, when I wrote a paper for my undergraduate work about prehistoric southwestern mural paintings at the University in Frankfurt, a topic which deeply fascinated me. It was the first time I was really captured by a topic, and it would become the best paper I ever wrote. After my presentation, my professor told me about an old friend who was the director of the Arizona State Museum, in Tucson, Arizona. He mentioned that every summer, the museum and associated university organize excavations in the Southwest, and I should think about participating. After all, there is not much Native American archaeology in Germany! I was intrigued, and even though I hated dirt, I contacted the university. There were two excavations going on during the following summer, so one of my friends from the University in Frankfurt and I chose to participate in an excavation conducted in northern Arizona, near Winslow; and this is how it all started.

During the summer of 1992, two young German women went into the desert, to Winslow, Arizona, of all places. We flew into Phoenix and took the two-hour shuttle bus to Tucson. The desolate landscape fascinated us, and we were amazed to see cottonwood fields along the road despite the otherwise dry and barren landscape. It was mid-May, and the dry air was hotter than either of us had ever experienced. The shuttle left us at the Tucson Mall in Tucson, where we were picked up by one of the project members. I was lucky to be invited to stay with my new boss, Dr. E. C. Adams, and I was very warmly welcomed by his lovely wife Jenny, who would later be my crew chief. Chuck, as I was told to call Dr. Adams, was in his late 40s, and his wife Jenny, with beautiful long blond hair, was in her mid 40s. Both were extremely hospitable, and they had a beautiful house with a desert garden, decorated with Pueblo paintings, baskets, pottery, and katsina dolls. I had my own bedroom and shared a bathroom with their thirteen-year-old son Nathan. I immediately became friends with the Adams, a friendship which I still treasure.

The next morning we went to the laboratory. The laboratory was an impressive, high ceiling room located in the beautiful and historic Arizona State Museum. Gorgeous ceiling decorations ornamented its foyer and the upstairs library. The lab was buzzing with people getting ready for the nine-week excavation. We two Germans stood around aimlessly. Somebody asked if we knew where the paper bags were? I had no idea where the bags were and what they might look like. We eagerly followed Rich to the basement of the museum to retrieve boxes filled with film canisters, stacks of paper bags, and other Rubbermaid boxes filled with curious materials.

It was burning hot outside, and loading the two big vans, one Suburban, and several private cars was not exactly fun. Everybody seemed to know each other, only we did not know anyone. One inquisitive museum employee heard about the two crazy German girls who were about to go north.

"Do you have any idea where they are taking you? Do you

know that there is absolutely no shade in Winslow? Do you know how much dust there is?"

No, I did not, not at all, but a day later we took the six-hour trip to the northern part of Arizona. Have you ever heard the Eagles song *Take it Easy*?

Well, I'm a standin' on a corner in Winslow, Arizona,
and such a fine sight to see
It's a girl, my Lord, in a flatbed Ford,
slowin' down to take a look at me ...

This basically describes Winslow: a strange agglomeration of people with different ethnic and religious backgrounds living in a long-lost town established in the 1880s. Though it is hard to believe it now, until 1960 Winslow was the largest town in northern Arizona. The so-called "Mother Highway," Route 66, was built in 1926 and used as a major pass for migrants to the west in the 1930s, especially during the Dust Bowl. It ran right though Winslow. Then, Interstate 40 was built, bypassing Winslow. The tourism-based commerce stagnated and many downtown businesses had to close. In the 1990s, a few bikers visited Winslow from time to time on their tour of Route 66, traveling from Chicago to Los Angeles. The old Route 66 still goes through Winslow, and sometimes brings rare tourist through town on their exploration of the romanticized past; sometimes it even brings German Harley riders through the little town. The travelers might visit the Falcon Family Restaurant for some of their delicious homemade breakfasts, or Casa Blanca, the restaurant with the best sopapillas. But that was about all you could do in Winslow in 1992, not counting playing pool with Navajo youngsters at a local bar. Two years later, the "Standin' On the Corner Foundation" was established, dedicated to restore downtown Winslow. Part of this work was to renovate and reopen the former Fred Harvey Hotel and Restaurant, now called the La Posada Hotel, and Winslow awoke from a twenty-year-long sleep.

Outside Winslow is the high desert of northern Arizona. And when I say desert, I mean desert. Not the beautiful and glamorous Sonoran Desert with all its varieties of cactus blossoms in all thinkable colors and shapes you see in various country western movies, which are often times filmed in the Old Tucson Studios. No, the high desert is desolate and its vegetation sparse, at least so it seems. No trees grow there other than some lonesome cottonwood and juniper trees, and unfortunately for archaeologists, also lack tree rings for possible dating. Many years later, when my husband and I revisited Winslow and camped at the then newly-created Homol'ovi Ruins State Park campground, my husband went to town to get some firewood. He returned with one of those fake heating logs, laughing. He had gone into one of the local stores to ask for firewood. The native Navajo lady looked at him in disbelief and asked somewhat annoyed, "Do you see any trees around here?"

That day, in 1992, we stayed at the then Bureau of Indian Affairs dorm, a dormitory for the Navajo and Hopi children who went to school in Winslow. During the summer months, the dorm was empty and we were able to rent it from the BIA. It had four main and two minor wings, and four big common bathrooms. In the center of the dorm was a big dining room or gym and the kitchen. The dorm had no air-conditioning and although during May and early June the temperatures would cool down during the night, in July it became unbearable to sleep. We would get up at 5 a.m. to be out in the field before the heat and come home exhausted at around 4 p.m.. I will never forget the first time I ever went to Homol'ovi II, the site we were supposed to work at for the next nine weeks. I could see my boss's pride in the special place in his lightened face, but ... I could see no site! As I climbed over rocks through the dust and stumbled helplessly after the other excited students, I could not make any sense out of "and here is a kiva," and "now we are standing in one of the three enclosed plazas" (enclosed by what?), or "here is a room block." It would take days (of course trying not to let anybody else know) until I could barely decipher the vague outlines of walls on the monotonous dusty ground. After a while, I could even see structures and kivas, which I had then learned were subterranean ceremonial chambers, still used by modern Pueblos. I could see the outlines of the three plazas and I could tell an ordinary rock apart from a worked rock used as architectural material. And I started to fall in love with archaeology!

I used to hate dirt; as a child I did not even play in a sandbox. So let me tell you a little bit about the fine, red, dusty dirt in Winslow. I bought a nice set of tan-colored (a neutral color I thought) towels in Germany for my trip; but after my first shower came my rude awakening. I had shoveled back dirt for almost the whole day and came back to the dorm for a well-deserved shower. An archaeologist with shovels you might ask? Right, usually we use trowels and even dentists' tools, but after each field season we do something really awkward: we fill the structures back in. You have to imagine that the structures we excavate are mostly underground now, filled in with sand and sometimes artifacts. But when you leave a structure open like this for long, it will deteriorate, the walls will cave in and you will lose any further information. Also, imagine digging a three-by-four-by-two yard structure with trowels! It takes a long time, and one summer is not enough. That is why we back fill everything carefully after each season. So when we come back the next year, what do we have to do? Right, shovel it out! And I can tell you, doing this at 90 degrees Fahrenheit and with no previous shovel experience is not easy. Despite the fact, that after two days you hurt in parts of your body you did not know you had, and you are very, very dirty.

The showers at the BIA dormitory were quite interesting themselves, considering the little sprinkle of water, with no adjustable temperature. And when you have long hair like me, you are doomed! But the best part is yet to come. When you think you are finally clean after scrubbing yourself with soap and shampoo as long as possible and then use your brand new, tan colored-towels, a nice surprise awaits you: the towel turns into a nice rusty red color. I did not have the feeling of being clean again until I came back to Germany nine weeks later! And guess what I did when I returned to the excavation the following year? I bought beautiful bright red towels!

And I did return, many times to come. The desert is magic, it is alive, it just takes you awhile to recognize it. Although I was so hot and so tired and so exhausted after the first few days, the desert, with its vastness and seemingly empty space, drew me quickly into its magic. There are the beautiful and snow-covered San Francisco Mountains in the west, the Hopi Buttes with their rugged, yet mysterious shapes in the north, the captivating Petrified Forest and the Painted Desert in the east and the breath-taking Mogollon Rim with its beautiful forests in the south. And to top it all off, in July and August the monsoon arrives with its curtain-like walls of rain. You can see them coming from the west, where the long-hair katsinas (spiritual and sacred beings known by Pueblo Indians in the Southwest) send the monsoon from after they return to the San Francisco Mountains following the Hopi ceremonies. When the rain comes, the desert changes nearly instantaneously and it becomes alive. Opportunistic flowers start blossoming and green grass covers the vast and previously dusty landscape. I found the following citation in a book by my favorite archaeologist and idol:

> *"I had never known so vast and so seemingly empty a world.... The combined vision of its natural grandeur, together with the imagined lives of the Ancient ones and the very immediacy if the struggling [Colorado] homesteaders, created for me almost a spiritual climate that has endured."*
>
> (Smith 1990:8, 1984:20)

This is what I had felt, and I could not have said it any better. You can really get addicted to the desert. I started to appreciate even the tiniest little flower or anything green suddenly rising out of the seemingly desolate dirt after a midsummer rain. I began to be grateful for the crooked shapes of the cottonwood trees, and you especially value the color green; green grass, the green evergreens to be found in the San Francisco Mountains near Flagstaff, just 40 miles east of Winslow.

This has been five years ago now, and I am still coming to Tucson and to Winslow, and this time my dream is to stay. Chris had gone home over Christmas and we met back in Tucson. It was a good reunion but the death of Jill put a strange uneasiness into the relationship. After all, the three of us planned to move together and spend the time in Tucson as three friends. Chris and I had, therefore, planned to live with our good friend Carole. As soon as we settled in, Edda's first letter arrived, and then another one and another. Every time a letter would arrive and I answered, it would take precisely ten days to receive the answer, exactly the time it took for a letter to get to Germany and for the immediate answer to come back. She wanted to know everything about me; being a little upset that I was so far away. On the one hand, I was happy to receive so many loving letters, on the other hand, after a while it started to put some pressure on me to have to answer that fast, and I started to wait a few days to a week to send the answer. Honestly, I did not know what to write in all those letters. Edda on the other hand, was eagerly waiting for my letter – which I can perfectly understand – and if did I not answer immediately, she would write a second letter, asking if she did something to hurt me or say something wrong, and that was the reason I did not want to write anymore. I never meant to hurt her and she never said anything wrong, so I tried to write as much as I could. Still I always had this pressure of having to write and this made the letters a little more unnatural. Being a student, well sort of, and excited to be at the university, I simply had other things on my mind. I had officially enrolled in my first graduate class as a visiting student, I could not afford more, and I was working at the Homol'ovi Laboratory every day. It was harder than I expected, but I also had time for fun.

Edda had also sent me copies of the letters she had received from the adoption agency after I had been adopted. They were the answers to her inquiries to my well-being. The first letter was dated February 3, 1969, shortly after my first birthday. From the letter, written kindly, yet professionally, I could see Edda's inner struggle, her pain and her regret. The letter informed her that I was doing very well and recently had worn my first little dress. It also notified her that my parents were very grateful to her for having given them a child, which they dearly love. The adoption agency had hoped that this information would bring some ease into Edda's mind. Edda had asked for pictures of me but her wish was not granted. Why would she want to be reminded of my existence all the time? They advised her to try to accept her decision and be glad that I have such a wonderful home. Edda was counseled to draw a line under that part of her life and to try to find a new beginning; basically, to forget about what happened and to start her life over again. Reading this official letter still brings tears into my eyes. Never will I be able to give her this time back, never will she be able to see me grow up, be part of my childhood.

The second letter is dated September 3, 1971. Apparently Edda had told the agent that she had married in the meantime and born another daughter, since she was congratulated about those two events. The adoption agent confirmed once more that I, who she called "Christinchen," a nick name for the name Christine, the first name Edda had given me, was developing just fine and my parents were still very grateful and would even stop by the agency from time to time to proudly show them my development and to show their deepest gratefulness to the agency who had given me to them.

Edda added a note on the bottom of this letter that she would receive similar letters every time she inquired about me. The last letter she had copied for me was dated January 25, 1973. In the letter the agent advises Edda to discontinue writing, since it was not appropriate to continue reminding my parents that I was adopted. You may imagine, reading this passage, that the most difficult part for me in finding my birth mother was how to deal with her feelings. An important aspect I learned from this experience was that no matter how old you are, you are someone's child, and in my case the child of two mothers. In Edda's mind, I was her daughter, then and now and forever. For me, however, she is "only" my birth mother and my heart fills with pain thinking how this must be for her; knowing that the woman I call my mother is somebody else.

Poor Edda, while I had my family and lots of friends to talk about my feelings, she only had one elderly woman- a very good friend who had known about my existence since I had been conceived- that she could talk to about me and her feelings and emotions. Once they even visited each other, and Edda was able to show her pictures of me. I was really glad that she had at least this person to which she could talk. They would write each other letters about me or talk on the phone when Karl, Edda's husband was swimming. He was retired early because of a health condition and thus always at home with Edda; even for her grocery shopping he would accompany her. Karl, who in the beginning did not mind us meeting, now started to resent the fact that I was there. And most of all, he did not want Edda to tell their daughters about my existence. Maybe because he realized the infatuation his wife had with me. He was thinking of his own daughters and did not want any disturbance in his family's life. I could understand that, but I was a little sad that I should not be able to meet my sisters.

I felt so bad that Edda was not allowed to tell anyone else about my existence. Reading her letters, I could feel her inner struggle. The only thing I could do to help her was to impress upon her that her family should always be the most important part of her life. I promised though, that even if we could not communicate for a while, I would always tell her where to find me, I would never really leave again. My emotions towards her now became those of guilt. There was this woman, who looked like me and who felt so much for me, whose baby I was, and I did not really know how to help her or what was the most appropriate thing for me to do. I was so glad it was her,

I liked her a lot, her kind nature, her soft voice, her diplomacy, her nice letters, but nobody had prepared me to how I was supposed to handle this specific situation with her husband and my relationship to her. After all, I did have parents. Edda wrote how happy she was that I had grown up with my loving family and that I was raised in the way she would have liked to raise her daughter. Edda was so thankful to have met me but yet so sad never to have seen me grow up. How difficult that must be for her, first to know that her baby had been raised by someone else and called someone else a mother and secondly, that now, when I had come back, she was not able to treat me like her daughter, to show her feelings, to embrace me and the situation and shout into the world that she had found her child. I could feel her pain when reading that I had been raised the way she would have loved to raise her children. Why had she never resisted her husband's wishes, I was wondering? The mother, who brought me up, would always tell my father if she did not like something. They would fight from time to time, but they had equal rights in the relationship.

At the same time, I had to encounter another emotional battle. Chris and I had to face Jill's parents in person. We had been to Tucson now for almost a week and her parents were eager to meet us. They had met Chris before, but never me. The e-mail I had received from Jill had been given to the police as evidence, and I had realized that not only had I been the last one to ever see Jill alive, I was also the last one she had contacted. Chris and I dreaded to go, but finally, we could not stall any longer. We walked the few blocks to their house. As we rang the doorbell, both of us had to cry. Her parents were strangely calm. Maybe all the tears that could be shed had flown, and there was nothing left but emptiness. We all sat in the living room and talked about what happened, what each of us had known, what we had felt about Jill and her life and how it had so tragically ended. The whole conversation took seven endless hours. Chris and I were thirsty and hungry but we were afraid to ask for something. I think Jill's parents' minds were absorbed with so much pain that normal human needs took a second place in their lives. It seemed that her parents just simply did not want us to leave, since we were the last people who had been with their beloved daughter. We did not know how to end this visit without offending them. We were the last people who had seen Jill happy and alive. The worst part was going into her room. As I had mentioned before, Jill, Chris, and I had planned to move together when we were back in Tucson, and now we saw her room, still as if she was alive. It had been hard to get her body out of Romania, her parents told us. Friends helped collect money to ship the coffin to the U.S., where her body was exhumed by her own professor. Jill had wanted to become a forensic anthropologist. The marks on her body had shown no sign of her trying to fight back, although she had extensive training in karate.

Jill had loved cow motifs, and her parents pointed to an inconspicuous box on the shelf while explaining that was why they put her ashes in a box with a black and white cow design. I almost fainted and Chris turned completely white, if that is possible considering her naturally fair skin color. I had not expected anything like this. In Germany, one has to bury a dead person, as a body or as ashes. You can not just take the ashes with you and keep them endlessly. I felt like I could not breathe. I was not afraid of the ashes, but the feeling of her body being in there after I had seen her in the window of the train playing the Rubic's Cube was too much. I had to get out. Somehow we managed to get back into the living room and a little later we were finally able to leave. We felt guilty and terrified. It took us a while to be able to talk again on the way home, and we started avoiding talking about Jill from that time on. It was such a painful experience, an experience that for me is inseparably interwoven with Edda for my entire life.

CHAPTER 5
Family Ties

Edda's letters now contained more information about my sisters, such as their birthdates, older and more recent photos, and information about what they did and do for a living. Christine seemed to be the most like me. She loves to travel, studies at a university, and loves to learn languages. In the following letters, Edda seemed more and more upset that she could not tell them about me, but she gave Amelie, the oldest, a sealed letter with all the information, in case something would ever happen to her before she had the chance to tell her daughters about me.

Mid-February 1997, my brother Christopher arrived in Tucson. I had been looking forward to his arrival, but Jill's death put a shadow on his visit. He and Jill's parents both thought that one reason she might have been killed, next to not getting married and thus not providing her fiancé with the needed papers to enter the U.S., was that the last sentence in that e-mail was directed to my brother, and might have been her death sentence. I hope that especially my brother will realize that he did not cause her death, but that Jill's fate had been sealed the moment she had decided to go to Romania.

Christopher was visiting for six weeks. The weather was great and he could even do some sunbathing in the yard, an activity not recommended in the midst of summer in Tucson. My brother and I have had a very special bond from the beginning. It all started when I was still an only child and I had to go to the hospital to get my tonsils removed. I was just two-and-a-half years old. It is a routine operation, but I was supposed to stay in the hospital for almost a week. In those days, it was believed that it was best for a child not to be visited by his or her parents. It was believed that separation anxiety would be even harder. There was a small window in the door of the room, through which one could only see from the outside in, but the children could not see their parents from the inside out. My mother came every day and it was painful for her not to be able to hold me or talk to me. The nurses were mainly immigration workers from the Philippines who barely spoke German and particularly did not understand the baby language of a sick German child. The children were kept calm using sedatives; thank goodness, times have changed. Today the parents can even stay with the children in the hospitals, even during the night.

There were about five children in the room. I even remember some details of the room; I remember that there was a girl, who seemed to be much older than me, maybe six years of age. I remember her having a bigger bed and eating oranges. The other children were small like me and had to stay in a crib. The room was white and sterile. Later on, my parents were told that those conditions must have invoked a shock in me, especially since I had already been in an orphanage for the first few months of my life. After only two days I had to be released early from the hospital. I had refused food or for anyone to touch me. Until I was a grownup, I was terrified of doctors or shots. One time, for a tetanus shot, three people including a nurse, the doctor, and my mother could not hold me to give me the shot. I had to be brought to a special hospital for mentally disadvantaged people where they finally succeeded in giving me the shot I needed after I had been bitten by a dog. My biggest fear, until very recently, was also of being abandoned. When I was released from the hospital and brought home, I would not talk or react to anything for many days. My pediatrician thought that I had lost my will to live! My parents were very concerned, thinking I might die. I was only lying in my bed staring at the ceiling. My mother told me that I did not react to any sound or motion. I was completely unresponsive.

During this time, the adoption agency called to let them know that there was a little boy born who needed parents. For a while my parents had thought about adopting another child, preferably a boy, so I would have a sibling; but now, thinking that I might die, they could not even think about having another child. My mother, who stayed the whole day with me, did not know what to do with me all day, so she told me about that little baby boy. Finally my parents decided to take me out of my bed and into the living room, surrounding me with all the food – I loved to eat – and all the toys I liked. And then, one day, I looked at my mother and said with my clear but weak voice,

"Where is my little brother?"

My mother started crying. That night, when I heard my father's car coming into the driveway, I ran to the door and put my hand through the mail slot (instead of a mailbox like in the U.S., this duplex house had a slot for mail built right into the front door and with little hands, one could reach right through it). When my father approached the door and he saw my little hand, he immediately knew I was finally recovering. Putting my hand through the mail slot had been our little game every night when he came home from work. For a few weeks he had missed that little gesture of love so much and he knew now that I was fine. A few days later, my parents called the adoption agency and confirmed their interest in the little baby boy.

I can even recall visiting my brother for the first time in the orphanage, where he was staying for the first three months of his life. I remember a nun in a black outfit and her hair covered bringing him to the waiting room where my parents and I were sitting. We could look at him and hold him for a while until he had to go back and we had to drive home until it was time to finally take him home. He was in good hands, since my father's aunt had been a nun in this order and was known by the nuns working in the orphanage.

A few weeks later, we were finally allowed to pick him up and take him home. I still see him lying in a bassinet in the back of the car. I was very proud of him, and excited to have a little brother. The only thing he had from his biological parents, who had been young college students, was a small pink and baby blue blanket. The funny thing is that he does not remember the blanket, but for me it represents an important event in my life. I still have it, and later used it when my children were born. The blanket today is in a special place, and if my brother has his own children some day, I will give it to him. My brother is very special to me and the circumstances about his adoption are a fond memory. When Christopher grew older and we had some fights, he would laugh and say: "It is your own fault, after all it was you who wanted me and now you have to deal with me!" We laugh about this a lot, and I could not wish for a better brother.

Christopher had fun in sunny Tucson; we toured Tombstone with my little red truck and even went for a small research trip with my boss to Winslow. Carole also accompanied us, and we took her car. We stayed in a nice hotel in Winslow with a pool, and after conducting our research at Homol'ovi we even went to visit Walpi, one of my favorite places in the world. Walpi is America's oldest continuously inhabited village and has limited access for tourists. Cameras or any other kind of media are not allowed, but guided tours are offered by members of the Hopi tribe. Walpi is one of the most beautiful places on earth in my opinion. It is this small mesa, accessible only through a natural stone bridge from the neighboring pueblo of Sichomovi. The view is incredible, and the combination of ancient ruins and more modern attachments, the feeling of the old spirits, is not easy to express. As we sat in front of the visitor center, waiting for our tour guide, two little puppies held our attention. One was apparently hurt, the other one just looking for any attention it could get. Two Hopi women urged us to take them home, since Maana, a Hopi word for little girl or maiden, would not survive with her injuries stemming from a car accident and Sewa, a Hopi name we were told means little sister, also did not have a very pleasant life ahead of her. Well, what can you do in a situation like this? Carole immediately asked me if we should take them home. Wow, is it this easy? You just find a dog and take it home? Being a German, I am used to months of discussion and arguments for and against a pet, the notion of just taking a pet, because it is there was entirely new to me. Well, what can I say? We came home with two little dogs!

Carole and I brought the dogs to the veterinarian and gave them their shots and Carole had Maana's leg operated on. Maana was doing great and although she would limp the rest of her life, she quickly got accustomed to that. One the other hand, after a week I decided to bring Sewa to the Humane Society. She was still a puppy, and likely to be adopted. I felt like I could not completely take care of a little dog, especially not knowing if I would be accepted at the university and could stay or not. In any case, I would also go back home to Germany in May for almost three months, to work at my favorite site in Germany. Who would take care of her then? It was a strange thing to bring Sewa to the Humane Society, in a strange way it reminded me how Edda had given me up to have a better life. I felt guilt-ridden about the little puppy, but only a few days later Ross and I went to see if Sewa was still there. She was long adopted. I hope she is happy. Even though you cannot compare a puppy with a child, feeling how I felt about Sewa, I could only start to imagine how difficult it must be to give away a child.

Yes, Ross and I had started hanging out together. While I had been in Germany, we had written a few letters back and forth, but nothing serious. Now, Ross and I started hanging out more and more. Ross was renovating his old house and we started to "date" in his bathroom, as I jokingly call it. Many nights after work and studying we would meet in his house and instead of going out like other freshly in-love couples, we would remove paint from his old lion-foot bathtub, then paint it again, and tile the bathroom floor and walls; and when I say tile, I mean four rows of one-by-one inch black and white checkerboard tiles! I loved "dating" in the bathroom though. It was a great time to get to know each other, have long interesting and philosophical conversations about life and death and the world in general. I really did enjoy it.

When the bathroom was finally finished – it looked absolutely gorgeous – we started moving our dates into, well ... guess where, yes, a coffee shop. Yes, Ross shared a big love of mine; coffee and cake. So we started going out to coffee shops to talk or study. The thing is though, that I actually go to bed early and Ross does not. It meant a big change for me, because sometimes Ross would actually call at 10 or 11 p.m. to ask me if I wanted to meet at a coffee shop. Not knowing that I had already been in bed, I agreed, jumped out of bed, got dressed, and hurried to the designated place. Then we would have our coffee and share a piece of delightful cake. Oh yeah, I did gain weight during this time and could not wait to get a break by going to Germany for a few weeks in the summer, to shed my surplus pounds. Later, when I came back from Germany, I finally had the heart to tell Ross that we could not keep eating high calorie cakes at midnight since I really should not be gaining weight like this. And guess what his response was? He was relieved, he told me that he had been gaining weight too, but did not want to say anything, since I seemed to enjoy the cake so much! Wow, sometimes it is good to tell the truth. We stopped eating cake but kept drinking coffee!

At the museum store, I bought Edda a little Apache basket, a symbolic little basket to place your sorrows in; she really liked it. I also told Edda that if I ever got married, she could come to my wedding, so at least she could see one major event in my life. She had felt honored, but asked if I thought my possible future husband would accept her. That was a strange question, I thought. What would somebody else, especially my future husband, have to do with my decision to invite my birth mother? I guess that was her different view of marriage than what I had grown up with. Later on though, that promise would become a major issue, which brought me lots of unexpected anger and frustration.

I sometimes almost felt ashamed to see how much Edda praised me and my "good heart." I almost feel embarrassed about this. Contemplating about this, I think that Edda was just so happy to have met me and discover that I was not angry with her as she had for some reason expected. And after all, she barely really knew me then. Of course, I am much more careful in what I say to her than to my parents, or people I have known much longer and who know me. With people you know well and for a long time, you do not have to be so careful all the time of saying something wrong or making a wrong impression. Edda seemed to not always be so happy with her husband's decisions and actions. In one letter she wrote the story about when their oldest daughter, Amelie, came home with a bad feeling about an exam. Instead of comforting her, he scolded her. How different that family was from mine. My mother would have never let my father do something she disagreed with. I started to have the feeling Edda was feeling guilty about having had an illegitimate child, and felt like she was lucky that someone married her and she had to do what he wanted.

One day, when I came back from the university on a nice 100 degree April day, a letter from Edda was there. I went into my room and lay down on the white metal bed, which sank down in the middle like a bean bag, and I opened the letter. It was over 85 degrees in the room, but you get used to almost everything. The swamp-cooler was constantly running, but seemed not to be able to get the temperatures in the house to lower than 80 degrees. I have to admit, although sometimes I dreaded to write the answer letters, I really got accustomed to receiving Edda's letters and I was looking forward to receiving a new one. When I took out the letter, two little pictures fell out. I anxiously picked them up. I could not believe my eyes: the first picture showed Edda, when she was about twenty years old and she looked exactly like me when I was her age! It was like staring into my own face! The second picture was her when she was pregnant with me. You could not really see the pregnancy yet, but it was strange to know that in that picture I was in there too. In her letter, once again, she writes how proud she is of me. She wanted me to meet my sisters as soon as possible and that made me very happy. It is so weird to have sisters somewhere and you have never seen them in your entire life. Who are they, would I like them, would they like me? Edda did not want me to be disappointed in them, so she added some of their negative sides in her letter. Of course I know they are not perfect beings, nobody is, I am not. I feel tears coming up my eyes and my heart aches. I feel so much pain for her, feel her hopes, her happiness and fears, all at the same time.

In May, a day before I left for Germany, I received another letter from Edda. This letter also contained a picture, a very unexpected picture. The picture was small, maybe an inch-by-an-inch, and on it I see a blond, blue-eyed young man smiling into the camera. The eighteen-year-old man, or do I have to say boy, is ... my birth father Ottie! If I had been angry at him before, I could not hold this feeling anymore when I saw this picture. He was so young, basically a child. A young American soldier out in another country, out to have fun, and most likely just as irresponsible, as most eighteen year olds are. Edda mentioned that his family was from Indiana and she thought that they had their own business. I suddenly felt more complete seeing his picture. I am part American, more than I thought. It was strange to see his face. Kind of strange that Ross is from Illinois and Ottie from Indiana. Not that far apart, really. In a way, Ross and I have a similar heritage. Somehow, having this picture, knowing where I came from, made me feel calm and relieved. A strange feeling of completeness overcame me.

It must have been very challenging for Edda to send this particular letter. Her writing sounded like a heartbroken woman and I finally started to understand that in a way she must still love Ottie! After all, this had been the love of her life, and I kind of do know what that means. She wrote that she had kept the picture for me in case I would ever contact her. She added that she had found similarities between him and me. No kidding ... that is where I got my ears from and the blond straight hair. But she also informed me that she did not want me to ever find him. He had left us, and did not deserve to have me back. Strangely enough though, she had written his former military address and his full name into the letter.

In the meantime, it was time for the university to contact me about my possible acceptance. It was a very turbulent time, and after some complications I was finally accepted to the university. I had received a full scholarship from Germany, which enabled me to be completely financially independent for the first year of graduate school. Ross and I went through a difficult time during this period. We had started to seriously fall in love, and the prospect of not being together was unbearable. It would most likely mean that our relationship would have to end if I was not accepted to the university. We did not want to get married prematurely, and a long distance relationship across the big ocean seemed unlikely to work. When we finally got notice that I could come back in the fall, we celebrated. We took his bright red, beat-up jeep to the Rincon Mountains and watched the sunset. I love riding in the jeep without its top around the mountains. Ross and Xenon and I would go camping in the wildest places you can imagine. It was wonderful. Then, it was time for me to fly back to Germany.

CHAPTER 6
Two Worlds

I was glad to be back in Germany with my family and friends and eat real, heavy, crunchy, German bread. I had just been home for a week when suddenly – while I was sitting in thc living room chatting with my parents – the phone rang. My mother answered it and then called out,

"It is your sister!"

My sister, really?! Which one? How? Why? I got a hot flash as I went to the phone. It was Amelie, who is the oldest of my half-sisters. Amelie told me that she had visited her parents the previous weekend. Everything was as usual up until the moment she had to go to the bathroom. A letter appeared from underneath the door. She opened it up and found my picture. She immediately saw some resemblance with her family, especially her Aunt Editha, Edda's older sister, and still wondering what this was all about, started to read. It was the first letter I had written to Edda. Amelie could not believe her eyes and when she opened the door, she found her mother waiting. They hugged each other and cried. Hearing this, I was close to tears myself. Amelie told me she had always wanted an older sibling, preferably a brother, but a sister was fine too. Oh well, thank goodness! She wanted to ask if we could meet. What a question! Of course I wanted to meet her! We made an appointment for Thursday the following week. Amelie would come to my hometown by train. I would pick her up at the train station and she would spend the day with my family and me.

I could not believe it! Amelie sounded really nice and, she was so excited to hear about my existence. I later heard from Edda that the two younger sisters are very close to each other and she, Edda, had hoped that Amelie and I could also get close.

Four siblings, especially four girls, seemed to be a better number than three, Edda thought. Amelie, who is only three years younger than me, told me on the phone how she and her sisters sometimes meet on Saturdays to go shopping in Cologne. They all have their own apartments, but live kind of close to each other. I imagined growing up with three sisters, hanging out, talking, going shopping together; that was a really nice thought. Nothing against my brother, I really love him dearly, but going shopping with girls is just something different.

I was a little scared when I went to the train station the morning of the following Thursday. Amelie had been so nice on the telephone, and I was hoping we could become friends, maybe even real sisters, whatever that meant. I walked the twenty minutes to the train station. There was a nice new little ice cream place close by, and I thought that before meeting my whole family it would be good for the two of us to get to know each other. It was a nice day, sunny and not too cold for mid-May in Germany. I was so nervous I cannot even remember the first time I saw her coming out of the train. I know we hugged and then walked to the ice cream shop. I asked Amelie later on how she remembered our first meeting, but she also cannot exactly remember the first moment. It is strange sometimes how our mind works in stress situations like that, even when they are positive situations.

I do remember our conversation though. We talked about what to call all of our new family members. I had a brother and three sisters, who, genetically had nothing in common with each other, except, that they were all my siblings. I also had a mother and a father, and at the same time Amelie and I shared a mother, but not a father. It was complicated, and in my naivety I suggested to make it easy and call all of them my siblings and to call Edda our mother. That conversation might sound strange to you right now, but at that time this was really an important issue, especially since Amelie was about to meet my brother, mother, and father. Amelie was tall, much taller than me, with brown hair, which fell in curls onto her shoulder. She had no bangs but a curled strand of hair fell into the middle of her forehead. Amelie smiled a lot and it made her hazel-colored eyes sparkle. She was very slender and wore dark clothing. It looked good on her though. She wore a black blazer with a black turtleneck shirt, which was enhanced with a white pearl necklace. I liked her style.

On the way through town towards my home, Amelie and I started trying to find similarities between us, physical and behavioral. We soon realized that, although I am the oldest, I am also the smallest of the four sisters and my brother. My sisters are all much taller than me, and unlike me they have darker, curly hair. Amelie was almost as tall as my brother. "Little" sister she began calling me pretty soon. At the ice cream shop Amelie told me about her life, and that she always had liked archaeology herself. Her father, though, had pushed the children into "secure" governmental jobs with good benefits; Amelie was unhappy. I told her that she could do everything she liked, but she seemed to think that because my parents had more money than hers, I had more chances in life. I did not agree with her. I had to work hard to earn money for my trips, and my parents had been anything other than pleased when I did not come back at the promised time, after I had gone to Argentina for the first time. I had planned to stay there for three months, but ended up spending six months, just to return again after three months in Germany. This going back and forth continued for about four years. Argentina, to my parents, seemed not to be the safest place for a young woman to travel, even though my father had lived there for some time in the 50s and had liked it. As a matter of fact, it was his beautiful slide collection of images from Peru, Argentina, and Brazil that made me want to go to South America in the first place.

It all had started when I came to Winslow for the first time in 1992, where I did not only fall in love with the desert, but also with Axel. He was my first real love. Of course, that changed when I met Ross. But once you have really loved someone, you do not just forget them. They are a part of your life forever.

I see a parallel in Edda's feelings for Ottie, my birth father, especially since they had a child together. Meeting Axel was a real turning point in my life. Not only did I return frequently to Arizona to excavate, I also started traveling to Argentina.

I loved Argentina. During the period of about three years I spent sixteen months there, most of the time excavating. According to Axel, I saw more archaeological sites than most Argentinean archaeologists, and for many of them we had to climb mountains up to 15,000 feet high. The sites were beautiful and very picturesque and usually located just on the highest tip of a mountain permitting a view across the magnificent landscape. Of course, at the time the sites were established, the marvelous landscape was less the reason for their location, but rather the need for observance in a time of common war and attacks, mostly from the Inca Empire. The experience inspired me to write a kids' story about children living in a local site under the rule of the Inca. My attempt was to make the children aware that these deserted sites were indeed the remnants of a once proud and prosperous people, and they could be proud to be the direct descendants of those people. The story was published in four parts in a local newspaper, and was even read in some school classes. Eventually, Axel and I broke up. It was heartbreaking but inevitable. Amelie thought that my parents had just paid for all my travels and escapades, but I told her that this was not really true. I worked hard to be able to afford all my travels and my parents had not been happy with me going to South America that often. They did, though, support me getting a higher education and for that I am forever grateful.

We walked slowly, talking, towards my home where Amelie finally met my family. She was greeted warmly and my parents immediately started trying to find similarities among us. My brother seemed to like her too, and we took pictures of the three of us in our backyard. Everything seemed like a dream and promised to be a wonderful relationship. Later on we went shopping in Ingelheim. Of course I also showed her

Charlemagne's site, where I had excavated, and we bought a nice, decorated box for Edda to store all my letters and memorabilia.

In my diary, I later wrote that it was difficult to express what I was feeling. It had been much less emotional than I had thought. Amelie was a nice girl and it was really easy meeting her and getting to know her. Amelie had the same major subjects in school as I did, and we had similar dreams as young girls, except I actually realized them. Amelie told me that I look the most like the middle sister, Sophie. But when she told me about Christine I felt some strong interest. Christine loves to learn languages and is studying abroad. Sounds familiar? Amelie loves Germany, she never had much money and is therefore fixed on security instead of finding the dream of her life. I almost felt responsible for her. I would love to meet all of them at one point, but the prospect also scares me a little.

Later, Edda wrote in a letter how much Amelie had liked me and my family and how comfortable she had felt meeting me. Edda was so happy and was hoping that she too, one day, would be able to meet me more often and be introduced to my loving family. But her husband was starting to get a little agitated. He did not even know that Amelie had met me, but he started to get worried about the constant letter exchange between me and his wife. Edda thought he might be jealous of her former relationship almost thirty years ago. Edda and her husband are married for twenty-eight years now, and I started to get worried about their relationship.

Then, just a week later, in the beginning of June 1997, I was back in Tucson to continue excavating at Homol'ovi. My body had just started to adjust to the nine-hour time change between Germany and Arizona and the 30 degree temperature difference between the desert and the moderate climate of central Germany, when I was coming back. The dry heat hits you like a baseball bat when you come out of the airplane wearing long pants and a sweater because it is always so cold on international flights. As I walked out of the plane I was reflecting on this short yet eventful time in Germany. Although I had met Amelie, I did not have time to see Edda again. Why, you might ask? Well, it is like this: on one hand I really want to see her, on the other hand I have a big family of my own who I grew up with and wanted to see, and some very, very good friends I also grew up with. To have friends, who have known you almost all your life, through good and bad, is the most wonderful thing you can have. I am very fond of my group of friends and a few in particular; and I foster our relationships. Another complication is that Edda lives eight hours away by train, and secondly there is the thing with her husband. Edda would calculate the time when my letter could come and then would try to get to the mailbox before her husband would realize there was another letter. And there is yet another family habit that is strange to me: in the first letter Edda wrote me to Homol'ovi, she told me how nice the letter was I had sent to Amelie. They had made a copy and each of them was keeping one. That seemed strange to me, and a little uncomfortable since I realized that I could never tell my mother any personal opinion on my sisters, since all of my letters would be shared.

My gypsy life started to bother me a little bit and the reason was Ross. We had seriously fallen in love and being separated first for three weeks, and then another nine for excavation really seemed hard. I had done the traveling life for five years now, and being almost thirty, I started yearning for a more settled life, maybe also a more intimate companionship. Ross came up to Homol'ovi twice with his old red jeep and I went down to Tucson once also. So what is the big deal? It takes exactly, and you can trust me on that, five hours and fifteen minutes from the Hopi dorm to Ross's house. That is a long drive, at least for me leaving at 5 p.m. on Friday afternoon and having to be back by 6 p.m. on Sunday for dinner. My boss was very explicit about this schedule. The two times Ross came up, we camped on the Mogollon Rim of the White Mountains. Why they are called white I do not know, but nevertheless they are magnificent! We took the rim road with Ross's jeep, and then camped out alongside the rim. You could see the rim drop and down below was pine forest as wide as you could see! The sunset is stunning and while you are amongst trees, you can see out above the rim and see the millions of stars and the Milky Way. What a romantic place for a new young love. We made a small fire and had mate tea. The mate I had brought from Argentina. It is a beautiful custom of sharing a gourd filled with yerba mate and drinking it from a bombilla, a metal straw. The tea is strong and has a high caffeine content. I, who was used to it, could sleep just fine, but Ross told me he could not sleep and started reading *Beowulf*. He finished the book but was startled by every noise the forest makes at night. When he finally fell asleep, he dreamed about a forest fire and woke up terrified; he still loves yerba mate though.

Coming back from the excavation, Ross and I took our first real vacation. With my little red pickup truck packed to its top and fastened with bungee cords, we headed for California. Our first stop was San Diego, which we both fell in love with. Balboa Park, with its abundance of museums and plants, is comparable to paradise if you ask me. We did not stay there, but continued up the rugged coast to Monterey, and further to San Francisco. In Monterey we wanted to camp on the beach, and found something signed "beach highway." Unaware and very ignorant of the meaning of this, we took this so-called beach highway, which turned out to basically be just a beach and not a highway, and we immediately got stuck in the sand- with the tide coming in! Ross thinks that I held my breath for about an hour. I could basically see my poor little red truck getting swept away by the sea. A park ranger, who was driving up and down the beach looking for stranded tourists, told us to let the air out of the tires. We did exactly that, and with a little shoveling of sand, we finally got the pickup free. Slowly, using the harder sand along the water, we got off the strange beach that someone had named a highway. We slept in a motel that night!

The following day we went to San Francisco! Oh, what a wonderful city. We must have walked across the entire city on that day. But what did we care, we were in love and enjoying every second of it. We even managed to get tickets for a live show, and afterwards found a nice authentic Italian restaurant with singing young Italian waiters! Then our trip continued to my aunt's house in Sonora, and from there to Yosemite, one of my favorite state parks.

Back in Tucson, a letter from Edda awaited me. The content shocked me for two reasons. She wrote that Amelie had been visiting, but that there had been no time to talk about me because her husband did not leave them unattended for one second. He was totally unaware of the fact that Amelie knew me and had met me, but he was so jealous in general that he could not stand having his daughter and wife talking without him being around. What bothered me was that Karl was not supposed to know that Amelie and I had met in person. Edda was terrified that if she told the other two daughters, her husband would divorce her. Her fear was so strong that she had already spoken to a home for the elderly, as a possible place of employment in case they would get divorced. That had really not been my intention. The letter I wrote her now had to be very carefully composed. I impressed upon her that her family should always be the highest priority for her; I would be fine. I did not feel rejected in any way, and would not take it personally if she had to temporarily abandon our relationship at this moment in time. It would not do her any good to get in trouble again because of me.

Poor Edda, she was in so much distress. Now, when she had finally found me, she was not able to express her feelings and tell people, and especially her other daughters, about it all. The pressure on me increased, and started to affect my daily life. I felt guilty and I knew I had to answer her letters immediately, which sometimes was a little hard to do, between working a lot and being in love. She would calculate the days of how long a letter would take from Germany to the U.S., followed by a response. Then she would go to the mailbox every day when the mailman comes, so that Karl would not realize that she still received frequent letters from me. I could never call her because of her husband. Edda further told me that Amelie, who was the daughter she confided in the most, would stand 100 percent behind Edda's decisions concerning me. Amelie told me later that our mother had promised her husband not to search for me, but she had never promised to not get in contact with me once I contacted her. Her husband had even told her once that she was selfish to have given me up for adoption. Selfish! To go through all that suffering of being pregnant and not knowing what to do, and then to have to give up the baby so that it would have a good and safe home. That is the most selfless act I could envision! Abortion itself is the more selfish act, at least in my view, since you would rather get rid of the problem than having to go through what Edda had to endure. I know there are cases when an abortion is necessary, and I would never condemn somebody who decides to go through this procedure, however, I would do whatever is possible to persuade that person to rethink this decision and maybe opt for adoption rather than abortion.

Edda told me that, on my thirteenth birthday, she had been at the house of the only friend who knew about my existence, the one I mentioned before, and she told her in a quiet moment that it was my birthday that day. Not a single day in my life, she wrote, did she not think about me, and there were endless nights in which she secretly cried out. She had never told her husband. Edda wrote that she was wishing for her husband to have an illegitimate child somewhere, so he could better understand the situation she was in. She added that she loves me just like her other daughters.

School started fast, and all the summer's events soon seemed to be far removed. After living with room mates, I was ready to move into m own place. I found a nice studio apartment in the neighborhood with a little garden and a terrace for myself. I loved the place immediately and moved in. Ross and I were not ready yet to commit to moving in together, and for me it was a great chance of becoming independent.

At the end of September 1997, I received a letter from Edda. She wrote that for the last three weeks she had felt so sad, and had cried about every little thing and then suddenly, on her late father's birthday, those unexplained feelings of sorrow had stopped. It was the day her brother had died. He had been in the hospital for three weeks, but his wife had not told anyone. She only called Edda after he had passed away. Edda was upset and disturbed; she would have loved to see him once more and to visit him in the hospital. Also, I would never get a chance to meet him. She told me what a wonderful person and artist he had been. I felt so sad for Edda. So many things she wished to do and now, even though I had come back, she could not live the life she had dreamed. She had gained her lost daughter back, but at the same time, there were so many restrictions and rules, that she could not enjoy me the way it was supposed to be. She could not introduce me to her parents, her brother, maybe not even to my other sisters, her sister, not the neighbors or friends. She tried so hard to be a part of my life even with the little things she could do, like making me beautiful little stitched runners and placemats. They are immaculate works of art and they are so intricate. I promised her that I would knit her a sweater some day. I am an excellent knitter and I used to earn money by knitting sweaters for stores. Shame on me though, it took me several years to finally keep my promise.

Edda is so thoughtful, she even made one of those beautiful stitched placemats for Ross. We cannot even use them because I am afraid they would get dirty. She sends greetings to Ross in every letter, and I think she is afraid he might not like or accept her. I do not know why, since she is just part of me and why would he not like her? She was hoping that next year, when I came to Germany with Ross, she would get to meet him.

I started sending my letters, especially letters containing things about Ottie, to Amelie instead of Edda. First of all, her husband should not know how many letters we wrote to each other and secondly, he started reading the letters I sent to Edda, so I could never write anything too personal. Our relationship continued to be really complicated. Letters were, therefore, sometimes delayed. For example, if Amelie did not visit her parents for a longer period of time, Edda would not receive a letter. Amelie started reading those letters to her mother over the phone. Not that I minded, but it is a little strange to write a letter to one person and to know it is read by two. Edda wrote more and more about her other daughters. I could feel how much she wanted me to meet them. She told me how much Sophie had suffered as a child. First she was born with a mis-shaped foot, then she had a heart murmur and later she developed arthritis. She suffers a lot, and went to several different doctors, with no success. I feel sorry for her, and wish I could help, but I cannot; I cannot even write her. Sophie also started to stutter when she was only a few years old. I wished I could meet her, but it was okay if that was not supposed to happen for some time.

Christmas was just around the corner. Ross was planning on going home for Christmas, and he asked me if I would like to accompany him. Oh, meeting the mother! I could not afford going home to Germany so often, so I accepted. Ross grew up on a farm west of Chicago. It is a grain farm with many acres. Ross's mother, Kay, is quite the character. She loves bright-colored clothing and is incredibly active for her age. She is about the same height as me and has bright blond hair.

Ross and I slept on a pullout couch in the dark wood-paneled family room, which had been an addition to the original farm house. The upstairs bedrooms in a home more than one hundred years old are too cold at that time of year. Ross and I had fun though. We met some of his friends, and went to Chicago. Chicago is an incredible city and I loved the feeling of its pulsating life. I don't think I would want to live in a big city like that, but it is fascinating going there for visits. Ross's family celebrates Christmas like Germans, with gift giving after church on Christmas Eve, instead of the next morning; that was nice. Ross's mother loves to give presents. I had never seen so many presents under a Christmas tree in my entire life!

I also met Ross's grandmother, Louise; a very kind lady with a big heart. We went to her little house several times, and I felt very welcomed. Her house was in the same town, but within the town limits and not in the countryside like Ross's parents' farm. The house was very small but lovingly and warmly decorated. I felt immediately at home there. The ten days went very fast, and it was soon time to take the flight back home, as school was about to begin again.

Tucson seemed to have the eternal summer after having been in Chicago. I loved my little apartment, but it was lonely without Ross. Then came my birthday: thirty years! Wow. I know for many young people thirty years seem to be the border between young and old, the magical line, the hateful unwanted birthday. I did not really feel any older. On the contrary, I felt in the midst of my life: I was happy and content with my life, my family, my wonderful boyfriend, and being where I wanted to be. Edda had sent me a special birthday card and apologized that she did not have any gifts for me. Oh, how silly of her; it was not about that. I was just happy that I found her and she is now part of my life.

She wrote, once again, that every day she walks to the mailbox and hopes for a letter from me. I had not written her in a while, and she was writing that she was hoping I was not sick or maybe that she had done or written something that made me feel upset. I felt some panic rising up into my stomach area reading this. What should I do? I could not write to her every week. I do not even call my parents that often. Although I have a pretty eventful life, there is not that much going on to write letters all the time. I was hoping that she would not always be afraid to lose me again, that I could make her understand that even though I did not write every week, I was there now and that she was part of my life now. Edda was happy that my mother and brother had written Amelie for Christmas.

I felt very proud of my family. How good they were handling the situation, and how generous and understanding they were. I had always been very grateful to my family, but now I was even more grateful and I understood how fortunate I was to have such a great family to call my own. I was particularly happy how honest we were with each other. Sure, we had our misunderstandings and fights, but we would not keep secrets from each other, or tell things partially to not hurt the other ones. After a fight we would always reconcile. We knew each other well and we did accepted each other's strengths and weaknesses.

Edda told me she wanted to tell the other two daughters about me when they were visiting on Christmas, but she was almost never alone with them because her husband was constantly around. She needed some time to tell them, time to explain, and answer questions. She was so discouraged that she had not been able to tell them this time. She had finally been able to read the letter my mother and brother had sent to Amelie, and Edda told me how she had to cry when she read it. She felt so relieved that I had such a great and loving home. Edda had always felt guilty that she had given me away. She told me how her husband was probably worried about her reputation, when friends and family would find out about her illegitimate daughter. He also was afraid how his daughters would react. In her letters, though, she also made sure that I he would have married her with a child, but at that time the adoption papers were already on their way and she did not want to take me away from my parents. She only wanted the best for me.

My life would have been very different if I she had not placed me for adoption. I cannot even imagine who I would be today if I had grown up with them and not with my parents and my family. It is a strange, thought, and although I do not want to hurt Edda, it was a thought I did not like very much. I had to wonder how my life would have been growing up with them instead. Would I live in Tucson right now? Would I have gone to Argentina, become an archaeologist? And ultimately, would I be the same person? One could argue that you are the same person and no matter what, the outcome of your life would be the same; or one could argue that things always happen the way they are supposed to, and as it is said in the *Witchblade*, one of my favorite shows, everything is connected and nothing is a coincidence. I tend to believe the latter. "The will is the link between the mind and the universe," as Ian Nottingham has stated so profoundly, and I do not lack will! The book *The Secret* is also based on this principle. A dear friend once told me that she never met a person who always gets what she wants the way I do.

Isn't that a strange thing to suddenly have two mothers: one who gave birth to you and looks like you; and one who raised you, knows who you are, what you think, what you did and do? It is hard to express how thankful I am to my parents. I know that this is not the rule, that not every adopted child had parents and a brother like me, but for me, this is who I am and I am grateful. Reading about Edda's pain of giving me away is really painful, though. I feel so much for her, but it is different. It almost seems as if the baby she is talking about is not even me. It is almost removed from me, since I do not remember anything of this. But she has those memories of me as a baby and I am this baby for her, forever. She did do the best for me, even though she had to suffer so much. How can I convince her that she did not act selfishly and that I am so grateful for her selfless decision? I wrote it to her again and again, trying to convince her that I was fine and thankful for what she had done for me. I could have not wished for any better life.

In Edda's letter, I learned more about my other two sisters. Christine was progressing in her studies. She was starting an internship in London soon, and would later go back to France for one more semester and then, most likely, to the former Yugoslavia to work on a humanitarian project. Edda was hoping to soon find an opportune moment to tell her and Sophie about me.

At the end of February 1998, my parents came to visit Tucson for almost four weeks. Although neither cared much for flying, the prospect of seeing me outweighed their fears. My apartment was a little too small for all three of us to share for such a long time, so we decided that they would live there and I would live in Ross's house. It worked out very well. Although it was the second-to-last week before spring break, I took two days off school and work to showed my parents the beautiful Sonoran Desert. The Tucson Mountain Park, the Desert Museum, and my favorite place Gates Pass, are a must-see when you come to visit Tucson. Gates Pass is a small pass through the Tucson Mountains; from the southeast you can see the vast expanse of Tucson and, crossing over the peak to the northwest, one is astonished by the most amazing Saguaro and Cholla cactuses, Ocotillos and other of the stunning variety of Sonoran desert plants. The Pass was built in 1883 as a shortcut from the Tucson Valley to the other side of the Tucson Mountains. While it is one of the most beautiful places in Tucson, it is also one of the most dangerous areas to drive. The road is narrow and winds around the edge of the mountains, which is one reason why it is so spectacular. There is a parking lot and a small ramada (a very common architectural feature in the southwest, it is kind of a roof) on Gates Pass, combined with some hiking trails from which one can enjoy the amazing landscape. When one leaves Gates Pass and follow the winding, narrow street down the north side one has the most stunning view of the Tucson Mountains with Kit Peak in its distance. Kit Peak houses one of the world's most famous telescopes, and it can take astronomers years to schedule the use of one of them. Visitors are welcome and one weekend my parents, Ross, and I went there to enjoy the higher mountains.

It turned out to be a good decision to take those two days off, since a few days later it started raining, and raining, and raining. It was the rain of the century, well in Tucson that is. My parents must have gone home thinking the desert is a rainy, moist, and most muddy place ever visited! And that comes from Germans, where it seems Germany and Great Britain compete for the rainiest place. My parents did not mind. They had fun. They quickly learned to use the extensive bus system in Tucson, and while I was at the university, they took the bus to places of which I had never even hear. It is apparently different when you come as a tourist, rather than living somewhere. Two weeks later, I had finally finished my midterms and spring break was starting. My parents and I took the plane to San Francisco.

My mother had not seen her sister in almost thirty years. My Aunt Maria and my mother are almost twenty years apart. My grandfather's first wife had two daughters, but she died when her children were still very small. My grandfather then married again and they had a son. Then the war started, and as a medical doctor he was called to his duty at the front. Story tells that every time he came home on leave another baby girl was born nine months later; that happened three times. The three sisters are close in age, but far apart from their older siblings. When my mother was small, her sister Maria married an American civilian, and when I was still a baby they moved to the lovely town of Sonora, California, where my uncle's family was from.

I was sixteen when I first visited my aunt. Since childhood I had always had this fascination with America, and finally I decided it was time to go there. I had written a letter to my aunt, whom I only knew from photographs, and introduced myself. I also asked her if I could come visit for a summer. I knit eighteen sweaters in order to pay for the airplane ticket. I was obsessed with knitting at that time, and within twelve months I was ready to go. The twelve hour flight was my first plane trip ever. I remember meeting a girl in the airplane who even took the same flight back as me, and we exchanged our experiences then. When I arrived in San Francisco, my Uncle Jimmie and my cousin Steven, both whom I had never met before, picked me up at the airport. My Aunt Maria was quite an impressive and domineering person. She was big and wearing a colorful muumuu. Although my German aunts had instructed her to only speak English with me, my persistence in answering only in German finally won. We went to Yosemite together and it is there where I had my very first Kentucky

Fried Chicken! Yosemite is a wonderful place and, believe it or not, it looked the way I thought all of American should look. Steven's wife had relatives in Los Angeles, and she took me on a trip to the big metropolis and also to Sea World in San Diego. I had a great time and met many people.

Although my Aunt Maria and I had some issues in the beginning, we both had the stubbornness most women in my family have, we soon began to like each other very much, and I returned four years later. When I finally moved to the U.S., I started visiting her frequently, and my aunt had developed into something like a second mother. We talked on the phone once a week. Now my Mom would finally see her and her husband, Jimmie, again.

We flew to San Francisco and rented a car for our trip east to Sonora. I love Sonora. The soft rolling hills with their silk-like grass looked so beautiful, like they were straight out of the *Little House on the Prairie* show. My aunt and uncle were so happy to see us and we had a great week. The first day was sunny and I showed my parents all the places I had liked so much, Lake Malone's, where I water skied for the first time, the fire station where my cousin Steven worked, and Colombia, the old gold mining town. I had been there so many times that I could find my way around pretty well. It was interesting to see my mother and my aunt together. They had not seen each other for almost 30 years, and had not had many contacts via telephone or mail before. It seems that they reconnected really fast, it almost seemed as if no time had past at all. I guess once you grow up with someone you have a familiarity that never ceases to exist.

While my parents lived in my little apartment, the gas went out. It was cold for Tucson, and damp, and there was no heat or gas to cook. My neighbor had a little child and needed heat desperately. Ross called the city and found out that the new owner of our triplex had stopped paying the gas bills. She had thought it was our responsibility to do so. But instead of telling us, she just turned the gas off! We were angry. The gas company turned it back on, since there was a little child in the house. The owner sent us letters with the notice of increased rent. It was time to leave. Ross asked if I wanted to move in, since his two roommates, Patrick and Hilary, were moving out to start a family. I happily agreed, and in March of 1998 Ross and I moved in together.

When my parents left I decided to write a letter to Edda's husband Karl. I did not date the letter, so Edda could give it to him at any time she felt would be a good moment. She could also decide not to give it to him at all.

Dear Mr. Müller,

Since about a year has passed since I found my birth mother, I would like to take the opportunity to introduce myself to her husband.

I am sincerely sorry if I have caused any trouble by coming back. It never got into my mind to come between you and your wife or your daughters. I also have a family, which I love. I grew up very well-protected and loved, similar to your daughters in your family. This is also the reason why I have not tried to find my birth mother any earlier. However, it is important for me to learn about my heritage. It was important for your wife to hear about me and that I was fine. After all, at one point, I had been a part of her.

I was so happy to hear that she had been married happily and had three more daughters. Since my parents could not adopt more than two children, I was delighted to find out that I had three more sisters. I have gained a second family and this is wonderful. Many adopted children, including my brother, are not as lucky.

I do understand that the situation for you is strange and not quite as joyous as for me, but maybe you could find it in your heart to give me, or better, give your wife a chance. I do not want to cause any harm to your family, but maybe you could accept me as a part of your family one day.

Sincerely,
Julia

The answer from Edda did not take long. She liked the letter to her husband, but did not know if she would ever find the opportune moment to show it to him. She wrote that, sometimes, she just did not know what to do. She just knows that she never wants to lose me again. Edda wrote that she could not even visit her daughters without her husband accompanying, an idea I had written to her, since he would never let her go alone. She mentioned that, even when her parents were still alive, Karl would rarely ever let her visit them without him. She assumed that he was jealous of them. He always wanted to be part of everything. She wrote that when Karl did not want something, he simply did not do it and there was no arguing. He is very stubborn, and to demonstrate she told me that Karl does not like the circus, so when Edda got reduced tickets she had to go with her neighbors.

When I read this I must think about how different the relationship of my parents is. They had arguments too, but generally each of them was "allowed" to do what they pleased. They would have never tried to stop the other one from doing something. To the contrary, my father was delighted when he did not have to go to family meetings, since the three sisters and all us kids where just too much for him. My parents had activities they did together, like playing bridge, but also apart. They both played tennis, but with different partners and at different times. My mother was a homemaker since my brother and I were born, but she managed the money my father earned. He would just ask for some coffee money here and there. He did not care about those things. He would not spend any money, not even for himself, so my mother had to do all the shopping, even clothes for him. He would have hated to have to go grocery shopping, while Edda told me that her husband even accompanied her there! I really love Ross, but I have to say, even I need to be alone sometimes. I could not imagine how it would be to have Ross around me all the time, twenty-four hours a day, as Karl was with Edda.

CHAPTER 7

The Summer of Meeting Everyone

At the end of February 1998, an unexpected letter arrived; a letter from my youngest sister Christine! I could not believe it! I was so excited I could almost not manage to open the letter to read it. Her letter was handwritten and four pages long. She wrote that it had not even been a day ago when she had heard about my existence. Christine wrote that she was visiting her parents and had arrived a day before her two sisters. That night before the arrival of her sisters, her mother had given her a Spanish children's story to read; Christine knows many languages, Spanish included. The author's name was Julia Theisen.

I had written the story while working in Argentina with Axel. We lived in a small Andean village called Tilcara, located in the beautiful Quebrada de Humahuaca, a valley cutting north-south through the northern part of the Argentinean Andes, connecting Bolivia with Argentina. Its sedimentary rocks create the most marvelous shades of yellow, white, orange, and red tones of sandstone giving the sparse desert landscape an almost mystical beauty. The site we mainly worked at was called *Los Amarillos* and is one of the truly most magnificent places in the world: "el sitio mas lindo en el mundo," as Axel had called it. Los Amarillos is located on a bright orange mountain rising up from the riverbed and ending in a yellow top, hence the Spanish word "amarillo." Its colors are so bright that it seems almost unreal. The site dates to late pre-(around A.D. 1200), and into post-Inca period of the *Quebrada de Humahuaca*, meaning it was first built by people local to the area and was later occupied and ruled by the advancing Inca during the 15th century. I wrote the story to bring history closer to the children in Tilcara, who were the direct descendents of the ancient inhabitants of the site. The story was well received by the local population, and was published in four parts in the local newspaper *Quivicha* and had even been read in school.

Christine had asked her mother who the author was, but did not get an answer. So she translated the story as she was told. When she asked again who the author was, Edda gave her my most recent letter. While reading the letter, Christine started to realize. It said how I wanted to finally meet all my sisters and mentioned that I wanted to know how my sister Christine was doing. At first, it almost seemed too unreal for Christine, and she was not sure for a moment if it was not all a dream. But somehow, the situation did not seem all that strange, since Christine had many dreams throughout her life of having another sibling somewhere. Still, it seemed so unreal for her, and she could not stop thinking about me. She was writing her letter to me the next morning while her parents went to the train station to pick up her sister. She wrote that our mother meant to tell her much earlier, but that in contrast to Amelie, she and Sophie did not come home to visit very often, and there was almost never much time alone with their mother. She wrote that the previous night there had been one of those rare moments, and her mother was able to tell her all about me. They managed to look at all my photographs and presents and letters together. Christine told me in her letter that in one photograph I even looked like her. Christine could not wait to actually meet me. She was leaving for England in a few days, but maybe I could come visit her there during my Germany trip the next summer, or she could come visit us some time soon. In her letter she also told me about her plans to go to Bosnia to work with an aid organization after her internship in England. She wrote about her father, who still did not know that now two of his daughters were aware of my existence. Christine thought that eventually, when all three sisters had met me, they would sit down with him and maybe that would change his opinion. She added that he was really not a bad person, and that it is probably not easy for him and he might feel like a third wheel. Christine thought that I should be part of their family as well as my own. She wrote how really happy she was to know about me, and was looking forward to receiving a letter from me, and to meet me soon. It felt strange to her to write to a person she did not know personally but, on the other hand, was so closely related to, and thus seemed somewhat familiar. Christine concluded the letter with the sentence that she hoped that I would like her letter.

Oh yes, I did like her letter. Her spontaneity, her openness, and her sense for adventures I really liked. I, too, felt kind of close to her, although I had never met her before. Of course, she could come and visit us; that would be wonderful! Suddenly, I had the highest hope that, in the end, everything would be fine. I was impressed with Christine's ability to speak foreign languages, apparently better than me. I really liked how uncomplicated and open she seemed. She spoke from her heart; it reminded me of how I might react in a similar way. There are definitely some similarities. I was so excited! Now I had two sisters I could write to, meet, maybe even hang out with. I was curious about her sense that she had another sibling. Amelie had told me the same thing; maybe intuitively, both knew. I also liked the way she talked about her father. How could anyone of us know what he really feels? On the other hand, maybe they should just talk to him about it and really ask what he was feeling.

A day or so later, a letter from Edda arrived. She wrote that I had probably already gotten Christine's letter, and Edda wanted to know how I felt about Christine. She wrote about how she and Christine told Sophie about me the following day. Sophie was not as excited as Christine or Amelie had been. However, she was curious and looked at all the pictures and read all my previous letters. Edda wrote that all three of my sisters could not understand Karl and his apprehension towards me. She and her daughters wanted him to accept me as part of their family. Edda seemed to be relieved that her three daughters were so positive towards me. They all liked the letter I wrote to their father, although he, of course, had never seen it. Edda was hoping to soon persuade him. She gave me Sophie's address, so I could write to her first, and I did.

I was relieved that all my sisters knew about my existence now, but I started to really worry about their father and their relationship to him. Writing to Edda in secret was one thing, but for them to all know about me and he did not seemed to be a little dishonest. But who was I to judge how other families deal with their internal problems?

Two weeks after I had received Christine's letter, a letter from Sophie arrived. I was a little nervous, since I had been warned so many times that she would be the hardest to befriend. Her letter was written very nicely, though, and there seemed to be no reason to be worried. She wrote how happy she was to receive my letter. She talked with Amelie, Christine, and their mother so many times about me that I did not seem at all like a stranger to her. She was surprised to read in one of my older letters to Edda that I had realized her new hair color in a picture Edda had sent to me. She told me she likes to hang out with her friends when school and work allowed the time, and she loves to go to the opera or musicals. She ended the letter by saying she was looking forward to meeting me in May, when I would be back in Germany for the summer. That did not seem so bad, and I was relieved. I really liked her and I actually liked the fact that she was a bit hesitant about being my sister, and that she wanted to get to know me better first.

The communication with Amelie was getting much more personal now. At Easter, she wrote me a nine page, handwritten letter, in which she told me about her new boyfriend and her worries concerning him. It was so nice to read her letter, feeling that she trusted me, and accepted me as someone close to her. It made me proud to be part of her life.

In Edda's next letter she again emphasized how happy she

was that all my sisters were so accepting of me, and she was grateful that we would stay in contact from now on. The only thing that started to become really difficult for me now was that I was kind of obligated to write four letters every two weeks. Not that I did not want to write them all, it was just that they shared my letters anyway, and there is not that much to say, really. I mean, I do think I have an interesting life, but not that many things happen that I can write four different letters every two weeks! But I know that they, well at least Edda, was expecting that I kept up with the conversation with all of them, so we would get to know each other better. I wanted that too, but it was strange, and I knew if I would not answer letters immediately, they would think something was wrong. So I tried to do my very best, but it did not work all the time. After all, I was in love, had just moved in with Ross, and we were renovating his little old house like crazy.

I think we moved our bedroom to every single room of the house, even for some time in the living room. After the bathroom was finished, we had started working on the front bedroom. We wanted to make it into an office. You cannot imagine the condition of this room when we started working on it. This eleven-by-eleven foot room had an outside door, a closet door, a door to the hallway, and two double-wide windows. All the woodwork was covered in about twelve layers of paint, which basically glued the windows shut permanently, unthinkable for an air-fanatic German! We scrubbed and put chemicals on the woodwork until all the paint was removed, and the beautiful, old, dark brown wood was visible. It was such a difference. We put a nice carpet in the room and bamboo window covers. It looked so peaceful and would have been, if not for the five-lane major street right in front of the window.

Edda was really curious about Ross and me. In every letter she sent him greetings and she kept asking if we knew if, and when, we would get married and where we wanted to live in the future. These were questions to which I did not have the answers. I was afraid that she was a little upset that Ross was

American, because Ottie had been. But she answered that it did not matter to her. She said that she had always thought about me, not about my father. I wondered if this was the truth.

In mid-April my father had a heart attack. After all the operations he had endured, he now he had a bad heart. He needed surgery, a triple bypass. My mother told me not to come, since the semester would end soon, and I was about to come home then anyway. My poor father, all his life he had been in good health. He played tennis several times a week, swam every week, and even took part in the elderly sports competitions every year. But then, three years prior, he had been diagnosed with prostate cancer. During the operation, something went wrong, and for a year my father was in and out of hospitals, sometimes for several months, having multiple surgeries. Finally, a year earlier, he seemed to be fine and slowly began to regain his old, active self. And, after all, they had even come to visit me just a short time ago. Now he was in the hospital again, with a life-threatening surgery ahead of him. As soon as school ended two weeks later, I was on my way. My father's operation went well and we went to visit him in the hospital. This always tanned and energetic man looked so small and beaten in the hospital setting. I was really upset, but could not really show it. It is difficult to deal with your parents' sickness and mortality; they are supposed to be there all your life. It occurred to me that adding onto my family, I would add to this kind of pain. After two more weeks in the hospital, he was sent to a rehabilitation center for six weeks, to learn to live with his new health condition, and to recover from all the surgeries of the past years.

My plan in Germany was, next to seeing my family, to meet with Edda and possibly her husband. Ross and I also decided to fly to London and meet with Christine. It would give us the opportunity to see London and to meet my "new" sister. Edda wrote me that our meeting had to be postponed a little because of her husband. Christine kept asking when they would tell their father, but Edda and Amelie knew that it would be hard, and the absolute right time had to be found. Edda wrote that she and her husband would visit his parents, and she wanted to persuade him to come to visit her parents' graves combined with meeting me. She did not know how to tell him yet, but since she had not seen me now in one-and-a-half years, she really wanted to meet me again, and possibly meet Ross. She was so excited, and so worried at the same time.

While my father went to the rehabilitation clinic, I worked for three weeks at my old Charlemagne excavation. I invited Amelie to be part of it. She was so excited. Amelie told me on several occasions that her dream had been archaeology as well, but she had not actually pursued the dream. She could not believe I would invite her to stay with my family and to work with me "in the field," as we call it. My wonderful mother invited Amelie to become part of our family, and we gave her a room of her own for the week she was staying with us.

I think Amelie really had fun excavating and seeing the life of an archaeologist hands on. And on top of it all, we had time to get to know each other better. Then, unexpectedly, Amelie's boyfriend showed up. It was a strange situation, since he was not supposed to know who I was, but he did not really ask either. He wanted to be with his girlfriend. Was I jealous? No, not really, just a little left out, I guess. Not that I did not want her to have a boyfriend, but it was not that we knew each other that well, and I wanted to spend as much time with her as I could.

Two days later, Sophie came to visit. We were a little nervous, Amelie and I, since Sophie was supposed to be the most critical one of the three; at least that is what I had been told. Amelie told me that Sophie was only coming because she, Amelie, was there too. But things went really well. Sophie also arrived with the train, and Amelie and I went to pick her up. Sophie and Amelie really look very much alike. Both are tall and slender, although Sophie is a little shorter than Amelie, but skinnier. I do not remember every detail of her visit, but I do remember taking our old, cute, black dog Sandy for a walk in the vineyards while the three of us, well Sophie and I mostly, were getting to know each other. Then we had coffee and cake with my mother and brother. I think it went well, and I really liked Sophie. It was okay, I felt, to be a little more reserved than Amelie and Christine, since, after all, we do not know each other, and just because we carry some of the same genes, does not mean we have to become best buddies. But I really liked her and was hoping we, too, would become friends eventually.

Two days after Sophie's visit, Amelie left. Christopher was kind of glad our lives were back in order. He and Amelie had a little fight while she was visiting. I was his family and that was just that. Although I was a little sad, since my nice, innocent, original plan of simply combining my two families did not work out. It is okay though. I have to respect his feelings. He did not look for his parents yet, and probably never will. He is my brother, and that will never change, and as for my siblings, he will always be the first. In the beginning I think, in all our excitement, Amelie and I went a little too far. We were so excited thinking we could combine these two families. I found out that this does not work. I learned I had to keep my families separate. It is not that I value them less, it is just that there are so many people involved, people with feelings, people who see me as being part of them. This brings me to the question "what is a family?" The people you grow up with? Biological relatives? People you feel spiritually related to? Your best friends? I know that blood is not necessarily thicker than water, symbolically spoken. I have very good friends who I consider my soul mates, and they are my family too. A relationship has to be established; it does not just happen just because you are genetically related. Every relationship you have is a gift that needs to be nurtured. I have several of those friends, especially Heike, Connie, Bärbel, and Mandingo. Mandingo, for example, is originally from the Republic of Congo. I met him in January 1993 at the dormitory of the University in Frankfurt, Germany. We became very good friends, and over the years, we established a friendship comparable to siblings, and eventually we started calling each other brother and sister. We would see each other as much as our busy schedules and travels would allow, and wrote caring letters to each other. This relationship would not change, even when he and I had partners and had oceans between us. We still care very much for each other and I thought that with my new sisters too, over time, we could establish a relationship that might become similar to this.

But let me get back to my busy summer of 1998. Ross finally arrived at the end of the summer and stayed for three weeks. It was his first time abroad, and he was very excited to see Germany and see my family again. I picked Ross up at the airport, and from there we immediately went to the rehab clinic to see my father. My father and Ross, during my parents' visit earlier that year, had become pretty fond of each other. They had the same kind of humor and my father, I think, was pretty happy with my choice of a man. It was breakfast time at the rehab center, and my father proudly invited us into the big dining room and showed us around. He introduced us to the staff and his fellow patients. He was so happy, he literally beamed with joy. After having a nice breakfast, we drove home.

Ross was really tired, but I just had to show him my cute little hometown first. It is so picturesque, so medieval. The streets are so narrow that two cars can barely pass, the Church's foundation stems from the 6th century A.D., and some of the buildings still inhabited are from the 16th century! Can you image? What a difference to America, where old is considered to be even less than one hundred years. How funny I always think it is to read an advertisement for companies, "serving since 1986." I guess age is relative.

I had to show Ross so much, introduce him to so many people. My friends all wanted to meet him and my extended family of course, too. So two days after his arrival, on a Sunday morning, they all arrived: my two aunts, my uncle and his wife, and my two cousins. It was a beautiful summer day. We had extended the old dark wood dining room table, which we only use on special occasions; usually we all eat in the kitchen on a corner bench. We had lunch – Germans eat a warm lunch, kind of like an American dinner – and it was a little awkward, since Ross did not speak German and although all my relatives know English, they are not fluent. Then we moved outside to the backyard with its gorgeous roses, and after some casual conversations had the obligatory coffee and homemade cake. Ross held up well, but I think he was glad when it was over.

The following day, a letter from Edda arrived. She sounded so relieved; she had finally found the heart to talk with her husband about me and my three sisters. She wrote that, first, he had felt left out, since they had met me without him knowing, which I can really understand, but since all three really liked me he could accept it. His explanation was that he had just been afraid that his family peace would be disturbed by my presence. It occurred to me that maybe Karl was not the way his family thought he was, and after all, I think most people in his situation would feel this way. In addition, he agreed to meet Ross and me on their way to his parents' house. Wow, what a wonderful development. I was so relieved, almost as much as Edda, to not have to hide my knowledge about my three sisters anymore. A plan was made to meet two days before Ross and I would fly to England to see Christine.

In addition to this event, another thing developed. Sophie and Amelie wanted to meet Ross too, and so they had decided to come to England one day after us on a bus, just for one day and meet Ross, Christine, and me! Wow, I have to give it to them, if they want something, they do it! Poor Ross, not only did he have to meet my family and friends, now he even had to pass the exam for yet another family. The saying "meet the family" became a whole new meaning if you happened to be involved with me! But Ross withstood the test well. Edda was so happy. Now she could write letters to me openly, and did not have to hide in the bathroom or wait until her husband went with the dog for a walk. She wrote that Karl, her husband is a really nice guy and she was hoping we would like each other. Edda also mentioned that she was hoping to meet my brother, Christopher, one day, and it occurred to me that she actually wanted to meet my parents.

Then the day of meeting Edda and Karl finally arrived. We planned to meet in the restaurant where Edda and I had eaten the first time we met. After that we wanted to go for a walk around the beautiful Nahe River Valley. It was a gorgeous day. Karl turned out to be a really nice man, and his English was surprisingly good. After all, he had lived and worked in South Africa as a young man, before he had met Edda. He is a tall man, as I had expected, with a slender body, and you can tell that he likes to swim and work out. His hair is white and full, and his eyes are bright. It was a beautiful day, we took many pictures and had a nice hike with their little old dog Lumpi. I brought Lumpi some special treats from our black dog Sandi, and I think it was a good move on my part. I was a little sad that, because of Karl's presence, I did not have much privacy with Edda, and thus could not talk about my sisters or my birth father. But all in all, I think the meeting went very well. I had prepared some more photographs of me as a child and of Arizona for Edda to take home, and she was happy. We had dinner after the hike and then parted.

Later, Edda wrote that she, too, had wished to talk to me more, but the opportunity had not been there. Poor Edda, she had waited so long to see me again, and now she could not say or do as she wanted. It was not as easy as I had imagined. I guess when I first contacted her, I had known that things would not always be effortless, but I had more related it to our first meeting. I had not so much anticipated all the things that would develop later.

The next day, Ross and I flew to London. That was awesome. Something went wrong with our seats and we ended up in first class. Let me tell you something about first class at British Airways: that means the best salmon you have ever had. The fifty-minute flight was almost not enough to eat all the delicious foods they had served us. It was great. From the airport we took a taxi to the hotel we reserved, and only shortly after we got there, Christine arrived. I recognized her immediately from the pictures. She was the smallest of the three sisters, but still a little bit taller than me. She looked a lot like Sophie, and I could see how those two would get along so well. Different from Sophie though, Christine is a real bubbly and openly excited person. Her eagerness to learn and to get to know me was almost overwhelming.

It was a nice and strange meeting. Christine did not only have to meet her unknown sister, but her boyfriend as well. That made our first meeting a little more awkward, but Christine's happy nature and our relaxed attitude helped it to be not as artificial. We went out to have fish and chips, we were in England after all, and then took a tour of London. Of course, we rode a typical double-decker bus and enjoyed the scenery from the top of the bus. London is a vivid city with lots to see, the changing of guards, Windsor Castle, and Big Ben included. We were tired after that trip, and went to the hotel to sleep. Christine went to her own housing and we met again the following day to continue our tour and to get to know each other better. That night we went to see "Miss Saigon." Christine had a blast, since she realized that I, being her oldest sister now, actually had to cry during the show! She thought that was very funny. Well, I have to admit, I do tend to get a little emotional when I see shows, or read books, or see a movie, but this is not what matters here.

The following day we waited and waited for the other two sisters. Their bus was late and we almost missed them at the appointed meeting place. Finally we were all together and had a peaceful, yes, cup of coffee at a nice coffee shop. There was lots of talking by all four sisters. I think all four of us agree that this was one of the best moments we ever had together, and it was one of the very few times, where we actually all were together. Then we went to Buckingham Palace and saw a little more of London. All four of us, five including Ross, wrote a postcard to Edda and Karl. After only a few hours, Amelie and Sophie already had to leave. That night, at the hotel, it all seemed like a dream to me. Did that just happen? Did Ross and I just meet all of my sisters? I could not help but wonder how it must have been growing up together and being part of their family instead of mine. I kind of envied them, having each other to talk to and be together. But I already started to realize that there was something that differentiated me from them, something I could not quite put my finger on. All in all, I would never want to change my family for anything, and even though it would have been nice to grow up with lots of sisters as friends, it occurred to me that not all sisters are necessarily friends.

Edda was ecstatic about the meeting. She wrote how grateful she was that we had all met, and how great it had been to receive that postcard from all four of us. Edda informed me that Amelie had finally told her boyfriend who I really was although Karl had been really against this. Edda was also disappointed that Karl refused to tell his parents about me. Well, I guess, I do understand him in this case. He does not have a particularly good relationship with his parents, and sometimes saying nothing or inaction is the right thing to do.

Edda was still so grateful to my parents. Almost every letter she mentioned them and how thankful she was. She was so impressed with how nice my mother had been to Sophie and Amelie while visiting at our house. Poor Edda, again and again she wrote how she had never been able to forget me and how she had always tried to imagine how I might look and what I would be doing. The last time she saw me I was this little helpless baby and now I was a young woman (yes, I do think thirty is still very young). She had been afraid that I would hate her because she had given me up for adoption. Far from that, I respect her, more than anybody, because of what she did, and because she had put my needs before hers.

After Ross and I came back from London, my father returned from the rehab center. That was good, so we could see him at home at least some more days. The time went fast and it was time to leave. I remember it like yesterday. We packed the little red car in front of our house and my brother was bringing us back to the airport. My mother came outside to say goodbye but my father stayed inside. All the surgeries and health issues made this strong man very emotional and he could not say goodbye to us outside. As I got into the car I looked up and saw him standing there at the living room window, which is a long window in the second story of the house. I knew, even though I could only see him waving, that he was crying. I felt like crying too, but tried to hide it. The image of him standing there, this man, who used to be so vital and healthy, seeing him so sad and so pale, almost shocked me. As we drove away, I waved out the car window until I could not see the house anymore. I just knew then in my heart, even though I did not want to believe it, that this would be the last time I would ever see him.

CHAPTER 8

The Vow

Shortly after Ross and I got back to Tucson, Christine announced that she would come visit us in two weeks! Wow, she is quick! Although I had warned her not to come in the midst of summer, she insisted that she loves heat and wanted to come right after her humanitarian work camp in Bosnia and before her semester at a University in France started. That was fine with me, I liked her and the sooner the better. She would just be there for ten days, and unfortunately only during one weekend, which was the only time Ross and I could really do something fun with her. Ross and I really wanted to show her a little more of Arizona than just the university, so we decided to take her on a road trip to northern Arizona the same Thursday she arrived, because the following weekend she would already be leaving.

As planned, Christine arrived on a hot Thursday morning and I picked her up at the Tucson Airport. Without giving her time to acclimate, we packed the jeep to go on our trip. A Jeep Wrangler, packed up to the rim with a cooler, tent, sleeping bags, and accessories, does not offer much room for guests. We squeezed Christine in between all the luggage in the middle of the backseat. It looked very funny. Christine with her sleepy eyes, excited, but having a hard time to stay awake and all our luggage on the open-roofed jeep. No, we could not have her ride like this for five to six hours. We decided to take out all of our luggage and repack it into my little Isuzu pickup, a much better plan. Now we had enough room for all our camping stuff and Christine could sit with us in the front cab. Finally we were ready.

We decided to take the picturesque Highway 87 north and

show Christine where I was spending nine weeks out of the year, and of course show off my knowledge of archaeology a little, just a little. Halfway to Winslow one has to cross the magnificent Mogollon Rim. North of Strawberry – yes, there is a town by that name – we turned east to the rim road and looked for a nice spot to camp. On the way north, it did not take long for Christine to fall asleep. Poor thing, although she had insisted she was fine and ready to go, the long trip and the jet lag took its toll. She looked so peaceful sleeping next to us.

We decided to camp at the rim to show her this incredible wonder of nature the next morning. We put up the tent and made a fire and had some mate tea. Christine went right back to sleep in the tent. The next morning we had coffee and hot cereal and Christine marveled at the beauty of the landscape. She had slept through the sudden change in environment, and could not believe all the forest after having been in the desert the day before. That day, Christine was very alert and we talked almost continuously; we talked about the experience of meeting each other, our childhoods, our dreams, our possible futures. I liked Christine a lot and we got along famously. Like me, she had that inner urge to move around the world, to experience different cultures, and to embrace whatever life would bring her.

Homol'ovi had been an important part of my life and I was excited to show Christine some of the work I had done. Christine was thrilled to get to know a bit more about her archaeologist sister. Poor Ross, Christine and I kept talking for the one-hour trip to Winslow. I had hoped for Christine to see an elk, but unfortunately we did not. Especially on Route 87 you can sometimes see those enormous animals, which look like leftovers from Jurassic Park standing with their impressive antlers next to the road. They tower a normal car and even Ross's jeep. The next day, we decided to see the Painted Desert and the Petrified Forest, which none of the three of us had ever seen. And just to make sure, there is no forest in the Petrified

Forest National Park, it is a desert, but ... there are hundreds upon hundreds of petrified logs in the most amazing shades of pink and white. There is almost no vegetation, and the emptiness and vastness of the landscape resembles a fantasy land out of the book *Eragon* or *The Lord of the Rings*. The Painted Desert is best seen at sunset when the colors of the desert illuminate in the most amazing shades of red, pink, yellow, and white. Christine sure was impressed. Like me, she was wearing sandals, shorts, and a t-shirt, and despite temperatures in the upper 90s she insisted that she really loved the heat. I really liked Christine. Her character was refreshing and somewhat innocent, and I loved watching her sparkly eyes when she inhaled all the new experiences to which we exposed her. The two of us also made sure that Ross took lots of pictures of the two sisters. We are almost the same height, although Christine is slightly taller than me. Her hair is a little darker and curlier than mine, but other than that, I really thought one could see that we were sisters. That was a very nice feeling.

Back in Tucson, I had the chance to show her the university, the desert, Mount Lemon, and of course, the Desert Museum, before she had to leave again. It was a great time and I had great respect for her to fly all the way to Tucson to visit me and Ross, whom she had just met.

Shortly after Christine left, the semester started again and we returned to our routine. Edda's letters kept arriving and oftentimes they included German archaeological articles she had found in newspapers. She inquired in detail on what I was doing in the field and in the laboratory, but I guess she learned a lot from Christine who had seen it firsthand. In one of her letters, Edda told me she had reread all the letters I sent to her and my sisters. She had copies of all of them. It made me feel uneasy, to know all my letters to the individual people were copied and distributed. I mentioned it to Edda and she promised me she would end the copying. She told me she had just wanted to know as much as possible about me. Edda understood there might be some things I just wanted to tell one of them and the letters were not meant for all four. But then she added how much those letters meant to her.

I was in a jam. I should have been happy about my new family, but now I felt bad. I decided to start calling her on the telephone from time to time. She could not call, since it was so expensive, but calling her from time to time was much nicer than writing a letter. Another thing started to annoy me, even though it probably should not have. When I sent a letter to Edda without specifically sending greetings to her husband, she answered that he felt left out. Oh my goodness, so now he was reading all my letters as well. I know, maybe I should not have made such a big deal out of it and it was nice that Edda always sent greetings to Ross. But Ross, different from her husband, would never feel left out if she did not mention to greet him. Those letters were for me and he would never read them. Now, do not get me wrong, there was nothing against sending greetings to Karl, but I just felt that my privacy was always invaded and I could never write the way I really felt, because there were all those unwritten rules I had to follow. Sometimes I simply forgot to write a greeting. Edda admitted that her husband always wanted to read my letters. To be able to express her real feelings, she had to write her letters to me when he was not at home, which was rarely the case. When I wanted to send her more private things, I had to send the letter to Amelie's address, so it could be given to Edda in a secret moment!

One night in September 1998, it was Friday the 25, my life changed dramatically. Ross and I had gone to the movies, which we did quite often in the summer – free air-conditioning, don't you know, – since we only had a swamp cooler. I remember it very vividly. We had talked about family members who had passed away. We came home at about 11 p.m. and there was a message on the answering machine. It was my mom. She sounded strange and wanted me to call back, no matter how late it was. Something was wrong. It was eight o'clock the following morning in Germany when I called back. My father had passed away about two hours ago as a result of a lung embolism! After all his sicknesses, finally it had seemed that my father was doing fine. After years of suffering, his death came suddenly. Ross called the airline to book a flight for me for early the next morning.

My mother and brother picked me up at the airport. It was a sad reunion. We went to the morgue and looked at my father one last time. He looked so peaceful with his hands folded on his chest and his eyes closed. It was as if he was sleeping, as a matter of fact, that was exactly how he always lay when he took an afternoon nap on the living room couch. My brother seemed so strong and he took care of my mother like a father. I was very impressed, but I knew that deep inside he was in so much pain himself. I was not sure how to console him, since I could not deal with my own pain. I remembered my father standing at the living room window just two months ago. Why did he have to suffer so much? Why had I not told him I loved him? I always assumed parents just simply know that we do. And then some day it is too late and you cannot tell them how grateful you were to have such wonderful parents, and you can not apologize for all the pain you might have caused them. The funeral was two days later. I love my family, but to meet them in this context was not what I had expected.

Traditionally, when everybody has left, the extended family will go to a restaurant or coffee house and have something we call a "Leichenschmaus," which means you eat and celebrate the life of the deceased. All my relatives, from my father's and mother's side, were there. On the way home, which I walked alone, I passed the cemetery. The cemetery is located on the foot of the hill where we live, and in order to get to our house, which is two rows above the cemetery, you have to pass it at its whole length. When I looked up to the top of the steep street going up the hill, I saw a triple rainbow. Somehow my heart filled with joy. I knew everything would be fine.

I spent almost three weeks in Germany. I asked my mother if she wanted me to stay longer, but since my brother was living at home at the time, she told me that she would be all right. Flying back to Tucson was not easy. It was hard to go back to work in the laboratory and focus on studying. I had missed classes and I had to keep up with the materials. I felt guilty that I had not been there more for my father during his long sickness because of my travels. But I was grateful that he had come to visit me in Tucson and especially that he had met Ross. They really liked each other from the first day they met and my father really liked Ross's cynical humor.

Edda wrote many kind letters trying to encourage, me but she started to worry since I had not answered for some time. I just needed time for myself. I did not want to think about anything or anyone and I did not feel like company either. However, I felt bad when I received Edda's third letter asking if she had written anything which made me upset. Edda also told me that she wrote to my mother and she hoped that she had found the right words. Edda and her husband were starting to plan a trip to Tucson. Ross and I invited them and they wanted to come and get to know the place where Ross and I were living. For Edda's birthday I had sent her a Native American silver pin, which she and her husband liked very much. I had addressed her husband as well and it made them very happy. The letter, which follows, contained a special letter from him for me.

Dear Julia,

I somehow have the urge to write to you a letter by myself and to tell you a few things.

First of all I want to thank you for the greetings you have sent to me in your last letter. I think you should know the following: I was delighted to meet you this summer. The way you behave and the way you put your thoughts into the letters are very kind. You seem to think with your heart, something which is very familiar to me since Edda does think the same way. I think that this was part of the reason why I wanted to spend my life at her side. Of course, Edda has many more positive characteristics which led me to give up my bachelor life and for her to be able to live with such a stubborn bachelor.

I want you to know, that if Edda would have kept you as a child, it would not have been a problem for me. I had already learned by then, that not everything in life goes the way you are planning it. Everybody makes decisions which later might turn out as a mistake.

After you had contacted her the first time I was afraid that our harmonious family life would be disrupted. Of course I am delighted that the opposite has happened. My negative thoughts were not right and I want to apologize for that. Of course you had every right to know why you were adopted and what had happened to your mother.

I am very glad that you came to us and that all our daughters like you a lot.

I hope we will have such a good relationship in the future,

Sincerely,
Karl

I was really honestly touched by this letter and very relieved. To be honest, I did not know if his family had really described him right, because it seemed that he really was an honest man who just wanted the best for his family. Who can blame him for that? I was delighted that he wrote to me and I was glad he began to accept me.

Fall, if days with an average temperature of 90 degrees Fahrenheit deserve that name, was coming, and I started to get my jeans out of the winter boxes. In Tucson it is over 100 degrees for six long months and when it finally cools down to the upper 80s and lower 90s you cannot wait any longer to get rid of the shorts and tank tops and little light summer dresses. The semester was coming to an end and I was busy writing papers and preparing for finals.

Christmas season had started and Ross and I decided to fly to Illinois again. We had both lost our fathers this year, but I had just been home and my mother would come in Spring, and Ross and I really wanted to spend Christmas together. We met lots of Ross's friends and visiting Chicago was a blast. Ross knew the city well, since he used to live there, and we had so much fun going shopping or just hanging out. Christmas though, was very sad and I realized I should have gone back to Germany. I felt so guilty for leaving my mother "alone" that first Christmas without my father. Flying to Europe costs a lot of money, but sometimes it is advisable to follow your heart and not the mind. Our instincts always know the answer, but many times we use logic and our mind to make decisions and then we have to pay the consequences. To this day, I feel guilty about going to Chicago instead of home to be with my mother on her first Christmas without my father. I learned that being selfish in the end hurts more than doing what your heart really tells you.

We spent New Years in Chicago. We stayed at Ross's friend Kelly's for the night. Kelly and his girlfriend, Julie, were invited to a party, but we went to Navy Pier and watched the fireworks over Lake Michigan. It was beautiful. Navy Pier was buzzing with activities and there were a lot of little shops and food stores. In one of the stores we found a llama puppet, which Ross just had to have. We called him Pepe and he scared the hell out of Kelly's two cats, Watson and Crick. The next morning Julie was ecstatic and announced that Kelly had proposed that night. I think she called half of the world after she woke up. I was a little jealous, just a little, because Ross and I had generally talked about possibly getting married, but he had not really asked yet.

While Julie was busy on the phone, Ross told Kelly about my birth mother and that I had an American father we had not yet found. That is when Kelly mentioned the Internet. What an idea! At that time, the Internet was generally available but not as widely used as today. Ross and Kelly worked on Kelly's computer, and guess what? When you have a unique name like Ottie Garrett, not Garrett, but Ottie, then you should not impregnate foreign women, because, I can tell you, you will be found! Within a few minutes they had tracked him down. Two with the same name that is, one – obviously the father – my grandfather I guessed! – and one the one for which I should be looking. There were several addresses listed, but a recent one was in Newport, Indiana, just four hours south of Ross's hometown! Can you believe it? There I am, traveling the world, just to chose a boyfriend who grew up in the same region as my very own birth father!

So what did we do? The following day, in a snowstorm, Ross and I took his late father's big, light grey pickup truck and drove south. What a strange little town Newport, Indiana is. It seems stuck in time about 100 years ago and forgotten ever since. It has an old town square and maybe a few hundred inhabitants. Just off a minor highway it lies hidden from time. We could not find the right house, but it was still an interesting experience. Ross got a nice new song out of it. He called it *Broken Town*. It is one of my favorite songs written by him.

Back in Tucson, I called my mother. We do that every few days, and she told me that she and Edda had talked on the phone for two hours! My mother told me Edda could not stop saying how glad she was that I had such nice parents. I was glad they got in contact, but I was a little, just a little bit, nervous about what they might have to talk about for two hours! I hoped my mother would keep the stories of how I went to the toilet for the first time or how I used to throw up every time we drove in the car or how I fell into the small stream with my clothes on, to herself. But you never know with my mother.

I had expected Edda's next letter to be happy, but it was a heartbreaking letter. Edda had mentioned before that, during the pregnancy, I never really moved inside her belly. Recently then, Sophie had read in a book that when a mother does not want a pregnancy or wants to keep it a secret, as in my case, the baby could feel it and consequently would not move much. I do not know where she got this knowledge from, but it for sure made Edda feel even more guilty than she already felt. She ensured me that she did love me and that, if at all, she only unconsciously did not want me to move inside her. I felt so bad. Of course I knew that she loved me and still loves me. I wrote the nicest letter I could think of, ensuring her that

I did not feel any kind of anger or resentment towards her, on the contrary. Unfortunately, I could not take her feeling of guilt away. I started wishing she could have kept the baby. Thinking about it almost seemed as if I was talking about "a baby" and not myself. I somehow felt removed from her story, I guess since I do not remember anything of that time. I only remember my parents and having a happy childhood. I do not remember the orphanage or anything before I was about two years old, which is quite normal for human development. This feeling of distance towards Edda made me feel guilty towards her. I could not really see her as my mother, despite our physical resemblance. My goodness, would these feelings ever stop, and could we ever have a normal relationship? What was normal in a situation like this? I really did not know. Edda compares me often to her own family; she says I have the same gift of writing stories like her sister and I am as good a photographer as her brother. Even that, which should make me happy, bothers me because I wanted those "gifts" as my own and not inherited from someone else. Why was life so complicated? Why can we not just enjoy the fact that we found each other, learn about each others' past and that is it? Life is so complicated. There are unexpected feelings, emotions, and circumstances, which we can ot account for before we make a decision, like contacting a lost birth parent. Oh, I would do it again, definitely, but maybe I should have prepared myself better for the outcome. But is that possible?

At the end of January, Ross and I went to Sedona for my birthday. It is supposed to be the most spiritual area in Arizona. We took his little red Jeep and booked a nice hotel with a pool. Sedona is a beautiful place, spiritual or not. Its rock formations radiate in all kinds of orange and red colors and the green evergreens only enhance the image. The faces of the rocks seem rounded and give the scenery an almost soft, creamy touch. We enjoyed the little town and the hotel pool and took the Jeep for a first spin around Sedona. Then Ross presented his present for me: he had researched my birth family from my birth father's side. It was amazing all the things he had found out: my grandparents were divorced and my grandmother had passed away a few years earlier. I had an uncle and an aunt and my family originated in Kentucky. Ross also found a new Kentucky address for Ottie. No wonder we had not found him in Indiana. He also found out that Ottie had published a book! A book called *X-Amish* telling about ten different cases of Amish families or individuals who have left the Old Order Amish and were shunned by their families as a result. I learned that Ottie's wife herself was ex-Amish. Ottie has six more children! One of them died as an infant, Philip. Four are boys, Chad, Monte, Joshua, and Matthew, and a "little" girl named Samantha. Wow, that was more than I had expected to learn, and I was satisfied for a while. Interesting though, that Ottie, as my biological father, would write a book, which comes close to an anthropological study, considering that I was an anthropologist!

Sedona is an amazing place. We took Ross's old Jeep and went up into the mountains. It was beautiful and magical. At a very remote place where you could see most of the beautiful red and yellow valley Ross finally popped the question. I was happy, but not really surprised. We had kind of talked about marriage before. Ross told me then that he had wanted to ask on New Years at Navy Pier, but he knew that Kelly would ask Julie that night and he did not want to seem like a copycat. We decided to marry in Germany, and according to German tradition, chose an engagement ring that we would wear on our left hand and then switch to the right when we got married. We decided to have my Hopi teacher, the now late Emory Sekaquaptewa, a very renowned Hopi elder from Third Mesa, make the rings using Hopi water symbols.

I felt like I was in Heaven, and the next morning called my mother and Edda. My mother was very excited. She liked Ross a lot and my father liked him too. I think she was happy too, especially that I was finally settling down. Although the U.S. was far away from Germany, it seemed much closer than Argentina. I asked my mother if she knew if nine months after the death of my father was fine with the Catholic Church or if there was a one year mourning period. Ross and I were planning on getting married in Germany in our old church in town. The foundation of this church dates back to the seventh century! I called Edda too, and she was also very excited to see her oldest daughter getting married. I was so excited and told her I was looking forward to seeing her, her husband, and my sisters at our wedding.

Edda was ecstatic in her next letter. She told me that she had been depressed that morning and she had hoped for a nice letter from me. Instead, I called and gave her the good news. I was her oldest daughter and would get married first. She already wanted to know if I wanted a nice decorative tablecloth, which she would stitch for me. She wrote that she had called Amelie immediately. By the time she called Sophie, my sister already knew. Amelie had been faster calling! Even Christine was already planning on getting vacation during that time so she could join our festivity. Edda was so excited that she would finally meet my mother and brother. My life seemed to be perfect and I was entirely happy.

Then something happened which I had not anticipated at all: My mother. My mother, who had been so tolerant with all my birth family members, suddenly became really emotional when it came to the wedding. She did not want me to invite my birth mother to our wedding. I was stunned. I had basically already invited them! She told me my sisters were fine, but it was too emotional for her to meet my birth mother for the first time at such a memorable and emotional day. She explained that, with my father having passed away so recently, she was still too emotional for a meeting with my birth family. And above all, she told me, this was our day, Ross's and mine, and people should celebrate us and not be distracted by the fact that I had invited two mothers at once. Although I was shocked, and to be honest, very surprised by her emotions, I did accept her feelings. I was her daughter, and this was our day. What should I do?

My birth family was so excited and I did not want to hurt Edda. I had to write her a very nice letter explaining my situation. I thought she would probably understand but I would really rather not have to tell her. I had told her that her family was the most important thing to me, just like my own family. And now I was faced with the situation where I had to make a decision between the two. Edda's response was kind as expected. Yes, she could understand my mother very well and she has already had the feeling that I would not be able to invite her. What a brave woman! She wrote that when she held my letter still unopened in her hand, she knew that the content would make her sad; the letter had seemed heavy in her hands. She told me that, of course, she had envisioned seeing me in my dress, standing next to me, but there were photographs, she added. The rest of the letter she talked about my sisters and normal stuff. I was so relieved and sent our handmade invitations to my sisters.

Christine, for her mother's sake, had decided not to come to our wedding, but was able to put herself into my mother's shoes. She said she had never lost somebody so close, meaning my father, and she could accept her feelings. She was happy that Ross and I were getting married and she was hoping to see us that year in Germany, or maybe in Paris where she was currently participating in an internship with Greenpeace.

The other two sisters though, did not react that kindly. They were furious. Sophie called and tried to persuade me, and Amelie explained why she was so angry in a letter. They were not at all able to understand me. Why would I go ahead and not invite my birth mother to an important event like that, after having started the whole "new family" business myself. My sisters and I were angry with one another and stopped communicating. Edda was suffering, but at the moment there was nothing I could do. My mother had to come first; to me my mothers' feelings had a greater priority than my sisters or even my birth mother.

CHAPTER 9

Of Happiness and Pain

It was a warm and sunny mid-February Saturday and Ross and I took his Jeep to bring some junk to the city dump. On the way home, I happened to see the sign for the Tucson Humane Society that jogged my memory. I suddenly remembered a dream I had the night before. It was about an orange cat. I wanted a cat for a long time and last night I had dreamed about an orange tabby cat just like him. I told Ross about the dream, and not showing any surprise by this revelation, Ross turned the car and we went to the Humane Society.

And guess what, there he was: a fluffy, three-year-old, orange cat. He looked just like the cat in my dream. I opened his cage and he basically jumped out of it and into my arms. He was an impressive and proud version of his kind with beautiful green eyes. And there I was, holding a cat, not exactly knowing what to do. I was sure my dream was true, but now this twelve-pound cat took me by surprise. Other people seemed interested in him, but he would not let go of me. He put his paws around my neck and held on. My mother, who was about to visit, is allergic to cats, but when I told Ross about my concern, he just said, "This is your cat, can't you see? We will handle the situation with your mother." We named him Puck after the *Midsummer Nights Dream* by Shakespeare. Puck and Xenon became best friends, and it is now 13 years ago and Puck is still my favorite animal, still sleeping with me every night. I cannot imagine my or our life without this furry little friend.

We rearranged Ross's house after his former tenant had moved out of the nice attached guesthouse, a common addition to Southwestern houses. The guesthouse, which was attached through a door between the two kitchens, had a big bedroom, which we had totally remodeled, a nice small bathroom with a shower, and a nice big eat-in kitchen that Ross had built by himself when he bought the house. The kitchen in his house was 70 years old, and needed major remodeling, so we decided to use the kitchen in the guesthouse for ourselves. Our dining room table, which I had purchased for my studio apartment, fit nicely in the eating part of the kitchen. My mother would sleep in the bedroom of the guesthouse having her own bathroom, and we would keep that part of the house cat-free.

In March, my mother arrived. The weather was great, as to be expected for a nice Tucson Spring, warm, but not too hot yet. March is my favorite month in Tucson with its cactuses blooming and the desert in full colors. Shortly after my mother arrived, spring break started and we packed my little red Isuzu truck for a road trip to California. We decided to visit my aunt again, and this time not to count on planes being late or bumpy and do it the American way – drive. It was a fourteen-hour drive and we decided to take it slow and stay in a motel for the night. This gave us lots of time to reconnect and talk about everything that had transpired lately. My mother and I shared driving, so after two or three hours we would switch drivers. I also introduced my mother to one of my favorite American fast food restaurants, Denny's.

We arrived in Sonora, California earlier than expected, and knowing that the side door would be unlocked we sneaked into the house. It was almost like in a TV show, my aunt, being completely unaware of our presence, was sitting on her new organ playing an old German folk song. So what did we do? We started singing along! My Aunt Maria was so surprised! After not seeing each other for almost thirty years, my mother and Aunt Maria had started a new relationship. They actually started feeling like sisters again, despite their twenty years difference in age.

My mother and I had a wonderful, relaxing, and joyful week in California. We visited Yosemite, one of my absolute favorite places in the U.S. We visited Columbia and my cousin Steven showed us the train museum in Jamestown. We went shopping in downtown Sonora and even met some of my Aunt Maria's old friends. I was happy about the renewed relationship between Aunt Maria and my mother since I loved both very much. Maria was not an easy lady to get along with, especially not for her two adult sons and her elderly husband, Uncle Jimmie, but I for sure loved her in a very special way. It was a beautiful trip and the best time I think I ever had with my mother.

Back in Tucson my mother and I had another task. We, including Ross of course, seriously started looking for a new house. Not that there was anything wrong with Ross's house, but it was 70 years old, kept as a rental for a long time, and needed major renovations. Its backyard was a sea of dust, but worse of all it was right next to one of Tucson's major five-lane streets. Ross and I were planning on having a family soon, and it seemed a better idea to buy a different house. We looked at lots of houses. Our goal was that it should be in the vicinity of the university, have a yard with some sort of plants and some shade if possible – we are in Tucson after all – and it should be in good condition, so we did not have to renovate. We also needed three bedrooms. It is not easy to find your dream home, either the neighborhood is wrong, the house is not designed well, or it has the same dusty backyard we already had.

Finally I found a picture of a house that seemed to be acceptable. Unfortunately, the showing could only be scheduled a day after my mother left mid-April. The following day our realtor showed me about ten houses. Ross was at work and wanted me to do the pre-selecting, and the house I had seen in the flyer was the first one he showed me. I could already tell him that we did not have to look at the other houses, but he insisted on showing me all ten. Nothing could compare to the first one though. It was located in the center of the city, but yet on a minor street, with an 18,000-square-foot yard, with trees. It was almost 60 years old but with beautifully-kept wood floors, an Arizona room, two bedrooms in the house and a cute little guesthouse with a bathroom in the backyard; perfect for a studio for Ross. And to top it all off, it had a Jacuzzi in the yard, something Ross and I had dreamed of for quite some time. I showed the house to Ross two days later and the deal was accomplished. Mid-May, ten days before my next trip to Germany, we moved into our dream house.

I left for Germany four weeks before Ross in order to plan the wedding and see my friends. Most things for the wedding, like renting a restaurant and talking to the priest, my mother had already done. I just had to help plan the buffet, and choose the flowers. We did not want a very big, elaborate wedding. I did not even need a wedding dress either since I had found a Mexican wedding dress about ten years ago in my Aunt Ruth's closet. It still had the tags and was never worn. It looked like a hippie dress and I had asked my aunt if I could have it. She gave it to me and since then it was stored in my mother's house. Now, finally, its time to shine had come.

I did not talk to my sisters during this time. They had decided not to come to our wedding and were still very angry with me. I just did not feel like dealing with this right now. I simply had other priorities at this time of my life. Having a second family, it became clear, was not all that easy. Despite all, I had sent Edda a wedding announcement. In her letter, she wrote that she had pleaded to her daughters to come, but it was something they did not want. I felt bad for her. First of all, that I had not considered the consequences and invited and then uninvited her and now that she stood between her daughters and me. I assured her that nothing would change my relationship with her, even if my relationship with my sisters was not as good or not there at all. She was suffering because of this situation. It all seemed so perfect in the beginning, with my parents accepting my decision to find my birth family, with having my sisters visit my family.

A week before the wedding, Ross and I met Edda and her husband. They were visiting his parents again and it seemed like a good idea to meet in the same town as last year. Edda tried to persuade us to come visit them at their house in northern Germany, but it was too little time for Ross and me so closely before the wedding, especially with Ross only being in Germany for three weeks. The trip to their home alone would take us an entire day and with preparing the wedding and guests from overseas coming, this was just not possible. In the end we met at exactly the same day and time we had met them the previous year! The visit was nice, despite the dispute with their daughters. Maybe it was a good thing that Karl lead the conversation, and the topic was not brought up. In a strange way it seemed much easier to write to each other, even though, if I wanted to write something her husband could not know, for example something about my birth father, I still had to send the letter to one of my sisters who would then either bring the letter at the next visit or read it on the phone! A complicated relationship.

I guess, because Edda seemed not to be upset about the whole wedding situation, my sisters started communication with me again. They still did not quite understand my point of view, but they all sent wedding cards for our wedding. I was relieved, and after the wedding we started working again on our relationships.

Ross and I had started taking dance lessons after he arrived. I had taken classical dance for many years, but although Ross is a musician, his dancing abilities are, let's say, limited. We took private lessons with my former tap teacher Uwe Kuenkler. Then Ross's mother Kay and Ann arrived. They stayed at the local bed and breakfast, which they really enjoyed. Before the wedding, we took them on one of the famous ship tours on the Rhine River, which local people only do, when entertaining visitors. Kay could not believe that in Germany we still had "Woolworth," since in the U.S. they had already disappeared. Most of her German souvenirs she bought there. But the main thing was that she had fun.

Finally, the big day had come. Well, that is the first day of two. In Germany, you must know, weddings are not like in the

U.S. First of all, a church wedding is not considered a legal wedding, so in order to get married in church, you have to first get married legally at the courthouse. The legal wedding can be roughly compared with the weddings in front of a judge in America. It is not a judge though, and you do not wear a white wedding gown, rather something simple yet nice, men however, do wear a suit of some sort. I wore a beige linen dress I had worn to my father's seventieth birthday. Heike, my best friend, and maid of honor, in Germany called a witness, had bought a beautiful beige and blue straw hat for my outfit. I happen to love hats and it looked gorgeous. Heike, of course, wore a hat too.

Let me, at this point, finally introduce my best friend Heike. Heike is tall and beautiful, with long blond hair and is always ready to smile and laugh. She can wear anything and it will look great! Her style in clothing is absolutely fantastic and I love going shopping with her. I always admired her will to succeed and her intelligence. She was the first female friend I had with a Ph.D. behind her name. I have known Heike since I was eight years old, when my parents, my brother, and I had moved to Gau-Algesheim from the twenty mile distant town of Bad Kreuznach, where I was born. Heike was in my new class. We had become friends, not best friends right away, but very good friends. Later on, during high school, she and I, and our three friends Astrid, Andrea, and Anne formed a group we called "Die Clique" and we are still all very good friends. With Heike though, I developed a very special relationship, later on, after high school. She was the one I would tell everything, would cry on her shoulders, and basically develop a relationship as close as a sister. I could not imagine a wedding without her.

The legal ceremony is a small celebration and only a few people were present: Ross and I, of course, our mothers, Ann, my brother Christopher, Heike and Vargus as our witnesses. It was a nice little ceremony. We had them make an international wedding certificate so we would be legally married in the U.S. as well. The ceremony is maybe fifteen minutes and after that you think, "This is it? Now we are married?" After the ceremony, we all went to a nice Italian restaurant and had a very good lunch. Then we went home to my mother's house and had, well, can you guess, right, coffee and cake, homemade cake of course! That was Thursday, the first of July. On Saturday, July 3rd, would be the church ceremony.

Saturday was an extremely hot day for German standards, particularly hot, since Germans in general do not have air-conditioning. Ross's wedding suit was black wool, poor guy. My dress was nice and airy. I did not want to wear a veil, but rather a wreath of flowers in my hair. It looked beautiful, if I may say so, and just the way I wanted it. My friend Guelay, a professional hairdresser, came in the morning to prepare my hair. I had to fight with her not to do too much, since I usually never do anything with my hair and I like it as natural as possible. At 2 p.m. then, the church ceremony would begin. We drove to the church in a red sports car decorated with flowers, which my father bought shortly before his death. Christopher drove. Ross and I went together, as is the custom in Germany. All the guests were already inside when we met Heike and Vargus and our two little flower girls, my sweet eleven-year-old godchild Anna and her younger sister Magdalena, in front of the church. Like me, they were wearing flower wreaths in their hair. They had chosen their own dresses, and looked absolutely gorgeous. In my honor, Heike had chosen a "hippie" skirt, long, wide, and dark green and a blouse with lots of lace. She looked beautiful; Vargus was wearing a dark suit.

There is no rehearsal for a German wedding and so we waited until the priest came outside to greet us and tell us quickly what to do. Anna's mother Bärbel, with her heart of gold, had lovingly prepared the details of the ceremony. Oh, what would I do without her? Then the ceremony began and with the priest and, with the altar girls and boys in the lead, we followed him through the long, big church. Anna and Magdalena walked behind the altar children, then Ross and I, followed by Vargus and Heike. We walked into the big, majestic church, which can hold over one thousand people. We had invited 75 people to our wedding, but more friends and neighbors had come to see the church ceremony. Despite all those people, the church seemed empty as we passed endless rows of benches. Finally, the front fifteen benches were filled with smiling, happy people. When we finally arrived at the altar, Anna, Magdalena, Heike and Vargus sat down in the first bench while we went with the priest to the altar, where we had special places. It was a beautiful ceremony, very unique. Ross even played a song for me on his black acoustic guitar he had brought from America. The same guitar I had seen him with first, when I visited his house with Patrick for the first time. It was absolutely beautiful and I was so glad I had heard him practice the song before, because otherwise I would have been too emotional. All the women in the church that I could see from my seat were crying, especially my mother.

Then we read our vows. It sounded so sweet to hear Ross say them in German with his American accent. It was very emotional. Then it was over and we walked out of the church. The guests followed us and everybody congratulated us. According to German tradition, my friends threw rose petals over us when we left the church. But if you think this was it, you are mistaken. Now we had to do our first task together as a married couple. Usually, the task includes sawing through a wood log with a dull sawblade, but since I was an archaeologist, my friends had prepared a sandbox for us to dig for a key. It was fun. The key opened a box with lots of fun things inside including diapers ... We never found the key, though, and my friends helped us open the box.

Then we had champagne in front of the church. Yes, ladies and gentleman, in Germany we are allowed to drink alcohol in public without hiding it in paper bags. Bärbel had prepared the communal drink. We had water too, though, sparkling water, as Germans drink. Everybody who had been in the church was invited. Bärbel, once again, had organized it and it was great! Then we all drove, one car behind the other, to the restaurant in the neighboring town. And guess what we are allowed to do? Honk our horns to announce the newly-wedded couple! At the restaurant we had, yes right, coffee and cake. Ross and I had to cut the beautiful three-layer wedding cake; but around it were placed about twenty different kinds of cakes, all made by family and friends! What a treat!

The restaurant had a nice party room with a place for dancing. The tables were set in a U-shape so that almost everybody could see everyone. I introduced everyone in English and German, since there were not so many people. In my nervousness though, I forgot to introduce my poor brother! He did not take it badly though. What a wonderful person he is. After the coffee and cake we all went for a nice walk to the historic area of Ingelheim. In the vicinity of the restaurant is a beautiful fortressed church from the twelfth century with double fortress walls. There, in front of the picturesque setting we took our wedding pictures.

After all the pictures were taken, we all walked back to the restaurant where now the buffet was being served. It was so hot that day that within a few hours all water, sparkling water, was gone. Germans do not drink tap water, so we had a slight problem. After the dinner, the party could start and Ross and I commemorated it with a waltz. Then the dance floor was opened. My friend Sabine's band played great music and later on Ross sat in (he was happy to not have to dance anymore) and played with them, while my family and friends danced. All my problems with my birth family were forgotten.

My friends had prepared some sketches to perform for us including something they called a German "fertility dance." As a costume they wore dish towels as skirts and homemade cardboard hats decorated with red balloons. It looked hilarious and was so funny. We left the restaurant at police hour, which is 2 a.m.! Our wedding had lasted for twelve hours and we were exhausted! Ross and I stayed in a hotel that night. It started raining during the night and continued raining all morning. In the afternoon the rain clouds lifted and we had a nice coffee and cake (now really, Germans do have that much coffee and cake), on my mother's terrace, overseeing my little picturesque hometown while opening the wedding gifts.

The rest of the time in Germany went by fast. A few days after the wedding Vargus, Kay, and Ann left and a little later Ross and I did as well. It was exciting to come back to Tucson, where we had a new house and were about to start our life as a family.

CHAPTER 10

A Growing Family

Ross and I returned to our beautiful house in Tucson mid-July 1999. It was almost unbearably hot outside this time of the year, but inside the house it was nice and cool. For Ross and I it seemed like an oasis. From the dining room window we could see the two-story tall willow tree with its lush leafy branches. Beyond the tree we could see the magnificent oleander bushes with their white and pink flowers. In Germany, I only knew oleanders from flowerpots and their size was nothing like those up to eight feet bushes, which can grow in Arizona. Our garden also had a water fountain, which I surrounded with geraniums, the only potted plants I did not destroy. Other than that, our yard was filled with desert plants, like Palo Verde trees, mesquite trees, barrel cactuses, or creosote bushes, and the most gigantic Eucalyptus tree you can imagine.

Unfortunately, I could only enjoy our little paradise for one week before I left for Winslow to be an instructor for the Earth Watch High School student grant program. Although I genuinely enjoy working with high school students, I missed my newly wedded husband. The two weeks passed quickly and I could finally treasure life in our own house. The bright green wallpaper decorated with big pink flowers, which ornamented the living room walls, suddenly seemed not to be as bothersome. Instead of painting, we were planning a big housewarming/wedding party.

I cleaned and arranged and prepared lots of food. We invited many people and the house and garden had to look their best. I worked so much that I had suddenly felt dizzy and almost threw up while trimming plants in the front yard. But the party would be the following day, so I continued working.

The next morning we prepared the last few things for the party when the first guests arrived. The party was a complete success, and it would be only the first of many awesome parties we would hold at our house. Lots of people came, it was an open party and some guests only came to briefly congratulate us, while others stayed for hours. I had forgotten about feeling dizzy, but the next morning I felt a little woozy again. Then suddenly it dawned on me. On Monday morning, when all of guests had left and the house was halfway in order, I went to the University Student Health Center. My suspicion was right. We were having a baby! Ross had been waiting anxiously for the results and I called him right away at work telling him the good news. He was so excited and so was I. In all those years I had thought I might not be able to conceive, it had never occurred to me that my own birth mother had four biological children without any problems! Seemed like I had inherited her fertility! Ross and I were ecstatic and started planning our life as a family. I calculated that I could even finish my last semester of coursework and the baby would come a few days after finals week. You cannot plan that better, even if you tried, I thought. I could then take some time off, being with the baby before I had to start preparing for my comprehensive exam!

I had sent Edda a photo album with photographs of the wedding. She was very grateful about that. I could tell, however, how painful it was for her that she had missed this important day. But she kept her positive attitude and did not want me to know. I decided that, to tell her the good news, I would call her directly. She was so happy and so excited at first, but in her next letter I could tell that this news had stirred up her old wounds. She wrote how happy she was to be pregnant, and how she had felt that nothing could ever happen to her or me as long as we were together and I was safe inside her womb. To give me away right after birth had been the most painful thing she had ever endured in her entire life.

Unfortunately, my answer letter got lost in the mail and Edda was even more worried that I would not write to her anymore. Poor Edda, she was always troubled. She could not understand that I had no intention at all to ever leave her again or to be angry with her for anything. I owed her my life and she had suffered so much for doing so. I was eternally grateful to her for that!

I wrote Edda that it would be nice if she and her husband could come and visit us after the baby was born. Edda was happy beyond words about this invitation. It did not take her long to plan a trip to Arizona with Karl for October of 2000. But that was a long time from now.

Ross and I wanted to celebrate our first Christmas as a married couple peacefully in our own house. We had a wonderful Christmas, without any stress of traveling. We invited lots of friends during the holidays, and celebrated the Millennium New Year in downtown Tucson with Ross's brother Grant and went to a big, big city-wide party. But since I had started to get bigger and was tired all the time now, we did not stay much longer than midnight. Other things seemed more important to me than a Millennium New Year.

The New Year started slowly for us. My last semester had begun and I had lots to do. One day in February of 2000, we had an unexpected call from my sister Amelie. She and her boyfriend had suddenly broken up and she was shaken and needed a distraction. She wanted to know if she could come visit us. Now? Sure, why not! It would have been nicer to visit after the baby had arrived, but if she felt she needed to see me now, that was fine as well. A few days later, Amelie arrived. I have to give her credit for being so adventurous. It was a nice visit, even though the heat and the pregnancy slowed me down a lot. I took Amelie with me to the university and to the laboratory, where I still had my student job analyzing pottery. Ross and I also took her on a short trip north to Lake Roosevelt, and went for a short hike to a prehistoric ruin. It was a beautiful day and from the hill we had a gorgeous view over the lake and the landscape. I think Amelie enjoyed her time, even though we could not give her a tour like we did with Christine, but she did see a lot nevertheless. We had sold my pickup truck and bought a used white minivan. Ross used his Jeep only for work, since I could not go off-roading anymore. It was nice to have Amelie in Tucson, since after the wedding issue we had to kind of start over with our relationship. We had a great week. Amelie slept the first few nights in the guest room, which now had to be transformed into the nursery. Amelie fearlessly helped to paint and even slept without any fuss in the living room for a few nights. Then, as fast as she had arrived, she left again, hopefully a little happier.

Edda continued to question her decision of placing me for adoption. It had consoled her a little reading about how happy my childhood had been, but she is upset that even after meeting Ross and I, her husband Karl still wanted to know every detail of every letter we exchanged. This forced her to write in those rare moments when she was alone, which usually coincided with the times when he went swimming. Edda told me that even when their daughters are visiting, her husband always wanted to know what they are talking about and cannot understand that there are topics which are best discussed exclusively among women. Edda told me about her father and how different he was from her own husband. Edda admired my relationship with Ross. Ross did not interfere in my life and decisions I made and we always had an open house for friends and relatives to come and visit.

On another occasion, Edda wanted to know if it was okay for our baby to call her husband grandfather. I was shocked! Not for Karl having a close, grandfather-like relationship to the child – that was fine with me. But Ross's and my father, the real grandfathers, had both just died. And to call Karl that just did not seem right. In addition, Karl had the same name as my father and that made things even worse for me. It felt like treason to my father. I tried to explain my feelings to her the best I could. She would be "Oma Edda" for the baby, no doubt, but her husband the baby would call by his name. The title "Opa," the German word for grandfather had been reserved for my father, who was cheated out of this relationship. Poor Edda felt bad for having asked that question and in her next letter she apologized to me. That made me feel uneasy, since it was a legitimate question, I just could not answer it with "yes."

A few weeks later, Edda told me in one of her letters that her sister Editha had given me a necklace with the words, "Gott schütze Dich," when I was born. The words mean, "God may always protect you," and they were written on the back of an angel. It was made of silver. Edda asked if I had ever received this necklace. At first I almost choked when I read this. Oh, yes, I knew the necklace. But I had given it away! But I had given it to a person who really needed it, and in retrospect I am glad I had given it to him.

During the last three months of my pregnancy, my blood pressure started rising. Since I had no other signs of distress, the midwives at the birthing center did not pay any attention to it. I had a little chest pain, but only after Puck had sat on my belly, which he enjoyed doing since I got pregnant. All of a sudden my blood pressure increased drastically, the decision was made to induce the birth at thirty-seven weeks. The birth was scheduled for the next day, April 27. The day before our baby was supposed to be born, Ross recorded a song with his friend in a recording studio, and when he came home that night, built our newly-purchased changing table. He finally went to bed at 11 p.m., but already a few minutes after he had lay down, I woke up with chest pain. We called the midwife and she told me to come to the hospital at once. My bag was packed and so we left immediately. At the hospital, they took my blood and only a few minutes later the doctors came rushing in: code red, my liver was failing, I had pre-eclampsia. Within ten minutes, the baby was born. I had to get a caesarian section with general anesthesia and as a result do not remember the first two days of our baby's life. Fortunately Ross could fill in my knowledge. He had been there for the birth and he was there to hold the little five-pound baby girl right after she was born. He told me later on that I kept waking up when I heard her crying, asking if it was a girl. He confirmed, at least five times! I do not remember nursing Carmen for the first time; I just remember that somehow I knew I had to nurse the baby. I felt very sick for several days after the birth. After four days in the hospital with women in the room, who had to watch *World Wrestling Federation* on TV right after they had delivered their babies, Ross decided to take us home. He could take care of us much better there than in the hospital, where there was always noise and disturbances. So we left. Carmen was little, but healthy, and she could come home with us. It was great to be in our familiar environment. During the first week, until my mother arrived, Ross took care of everything. I had not changed a single diaper within the first week of Carmen's life! The only thing I had to do was feed our little baby.

I had sent the first picture of Carmen, which was taken at the hospital, to Edda immediately when I felt better. The photograph is funny. Carmen looks like a little wiggle worm, as we called her, pink and small, with red, long, narrow feet. She seemed – and by the way still is – the most beautiful creature in the world! I had addressed the letter to Oma Edda and as the addressee I had put Carmen's name. Edda was overjoyed that her grandchild would really be calling her that. She wrote that her husband did not comment at all on this, about which she was upset. I was not sure if that was a good or a bad sign. Edda was so proud and pointed out the similarities between Carmen and me, when I was that little. Unfortunately, she was not allowed to show the pictures of Carmen to anybody or tell anyone that she was a proud grandmother. My goodness, now she had not only lost a child, she was even denied the joy of being a grandmother. Why she never stood up to her husband, I do not know. I got the impression that she felt she was in his debt, since he had married her, despite her having had an illegitimate child. Their relationship really befuddled me. On one hand, Karl was this nice guy, who I am sure, was deeply in love with his wife. On the other hand, he was so repressing and oppressive to her.

A week after Carmen's birth, Ross went to the airport to pick up my mother. I was still very weak and stayed home with Carmen. I was so excited to see my mother. I could not wait for her to meet her little granddaughter and also, to be honest, to help me a little with the baby and the house. Ross had to go back to work and my mother would stay with us for five weeks. It was a special moment in my mother's life to see her little granddaughter. My mother, with her sixty years, looked young with her new short haircut, even though her hair was now completely whitish-gray. I like her hair color, and I admire that she does not hide it. I personally do not like short hair that much, but to my mother it fit really well. My mother stood in front of the crib and admired Carmen. She herself had never bore a child and I was already over two months old when I came to my parents. Therefore, Carmen, with her five pounds, seemed incredibly small and fragile to my mother.

After a week of adjustment and of caring lovingly for her little granddaughter, my mother faced the task of thoroughly cleaning our house. I do not think the house was ever that clean again. I am not sure if there is ever a point where a daughter, no matter how old, could ever clean well enough for her mother. Ten days after the birth we started going for walks with Carmen in my beautiful forest-green Swedish stroller. The scar still hurt, but I could hold on to the stroller. However, the heat, which at this point had reached the 105 degree Fahrenheit mark, made walking with an infant almost a torture. My mother enjoyed being a grandmother or "Omi," the German word for grandmother. She and Carmen started a bonding, which until now has not subsided.

Being a mother was quite overwhelming for me at first. I started thinking that I could never again leave the house. To get the baby ready to go anywhere, to put her into the car seat, drive to the store, get her back out, and then back into the car, seemed to be an impossible task. Then my mother left and my panic proved unfounded, and I managed quite well. A few weeks later Heike arrived to meet her new godchild.

Heike had just finished her Ph.D. in Neurobiology and since in Germany, we do not have a graduation ceremony with regalia, and I bought her the appropriate outfit from my university. The usual black outfit was purple this year to commemorate the millennium. Heike had to pose in front of the old Student Union, a particularly beautiful building and the first one of the University of Arizona. We took lots of pictures, even some with her and Carmen. Having Heike there was great. Naturally, we had to talk about lots of stuff and it was great to converse in my native tongue about everything that had happened recently. You find friends later in life, good friends, but the best friends I have come from my childhood or my time at the university. It is just something different, someone who just knows all about you, knows what you went through in the different phases of your life. I do not know if my sisters and I could ever reach such a point of closeness, even if we tried.

I sent more photographs to Edda and my three sisters. They were really proud to be aunts, and I think our little argument about the wedding was long forgotten, thank goodness. Edda wrote that even Karl was fond of the similarities between Carmen and her aunts when they were babies. It is funny, while Kay, Ross's mother seemed to see distinct similarities in Carmen with her family, so did Edda and her family. I guess in a baby's features you can find similarities to almost everyone. I for one was sure Carmen looked definitely like me!

That year we had lots of visitors in our house in Tucson, in fact we called it the "year of visitors." A little after Heike had left, my brother, Carmen's godfather, arrived. My brother, as I have mentioned before, is a very generous person and his first task was to make sure that Carmen had the best car seat for a growing baby. Within her six months she had outgrown her infant car seat. Secondly, Christopher bought us the best baby backpack money could buy, with a sunroof, of course. As students, these were really generous gifts, and we were very grateful. Christopher was proud to be an uncle and godfather. He loved Carmen and handled her quite naturally.

Two weeks after Christopher left, Edda and her husband arrived. I am telling you, it was the year of visits! Edda was so excited. She wrote that she could not wait to see the places I had told her about, like the beautiful Mission of *San Xavier del Bac* or the Desert Museum. We picked her and Karl up at the airport during the middle of October. I told her that this would be the best time to come, since for German standards October still had summer temperatures, but for us it was the time when the weather had started to cool down a little; and by cooled down I mean in the 90s or maybe even upper 80s if we were lucky. Edda and her husband stayed for almost three weeks. I was nervous to have them living with us for so long, after all, I had only met Karl twice and Edda three times before. My worry proved wrong though and we had a great time together. Unfortunately, but expected, Karl barely gave Edda and me time to talk in private. The only time we had for ourselves was when he lay down some rare afternoons, when his back was bothering him. While he was sleeping Edda and I had a little time to talk about Ottie and what had happened thirty-three years ago. I got the distinct feeling that Edda, maybe even unconsciously, still felt a lot for Ottie, even if she hated him for what he had done to her and me. Although she repeatedly told me that Ottie had died for her the day he had disappeared, he had been her first big love, just like Axel had been for me. I understand that all the events following her announcement that she was pregnant had never been resolved between them. I felt that, although she wanted to hate Ottie so much, she could not. She always wondered "what would have been if..." In my opinion, nobody should ever ask this question, it keeps you from living your life as it is and enjoying and experiencing it the way it is. We live right now and right here. I did not have the heart to tell her that I had started to research Ottie, and I told myself that unless I actually contacted him, there was no reason to make her worry. I had to wonder though, if there would ever be the time when the two of them would get the chance to talk to each other, and hopefully resolve these old events. I was starting to question why he had left so suddenly after Edda had announced that she was expecting.

Edda, Karl, Ross and I did a lot of exploring the scenery during their visit, like hiking on Mount Lemon, a retreat from the desert with its lush pine trees and cool air and its stunning view over Tucson. We went to Tucson Mountain Park and the Desert Museum to see the beautiful Sonoran Desert in all its might. We also visited San Xavier to learn about the early history of Tucson and, of course, we went to my favorite Arizona State Museum, where a bowl I helped find and glued together is exhibited. I basically could live in that museum; it is like home to me. My laboratory, where I used to work, is right in the museum. For lunch, I would go to the little seating area of the exhibit and eat my sandwich, listening to the wondrous sounds of Yaqui music from the exhibit. The exhibit is about ten of the Southwestern ethnic groups with their past and present life, and their views on their future. It is well designed and laid out, and of course includes an exposé of Homol'ovi. No wonder I feel at home there.

Then it was Halloween, and for those who do not know, in those days Germany did not celebrate Halloween. Therefore, for Edda and her husband this was a very cultural experience. We had one of our famous parties and invited lots of friends of various cultural backgrounds along with lots of children. It was a wonderful party, centered around the babies of course. One of the advantages of living in Tucson is that no matter when you have a party, you can always celebrate outside. People are used to the heat and in the mild winters everybody enjoys the outdoors. Edda's husband was in Heaven. He could speak English fairly well, and had fun talking to all the different people. Edda, on the other hand, enjoyed having so many babies and children around, and being treated as Carmen's grandmother was the height of her trip. She told me later on how much they had enjoyed the time with us, and that her husband was telling everyone, even his parents, how great it was and how nice we were. But of course, to Edda's pain, he said that they had been visiting some distant "friends" and not her daughter and grandchild. In all his stories, my real identity was never revealed.

Shortly after Edda and her husband left, Kay and Louise, Ross's mother and grandmother, arrived. The weather finally cooled down, but for Illinois November weather standard, 80 degrees Fahrenheit was summer. Great-Grandma Louise had helped Ross and I financially when we bought this beautiful house, and we were glad to welcome her into our home. Kay and Louise had not seen Carmen yet. They were so excited and Carmen, being a very friendly baby, immediately took to the two of them. Ross was especially happy about his grandmother being here, because her health had recently started to be frail. She had a very high blood iron count and was just not feeling herself. With her eighty-four years she was still living by herself in her little house, in which she had once lived with her daughter, raising her as a single mother, after a divorce.

Louise has a very strong personality; she is a very kind and gentle person with a big open heart. We both felt grateful for her being here. We took a beautiful four generation picture of her, Ross's mother, Ross, and Carmen, all sitting under the big Palo Verde tree in our backyard. Louise got to hold Carmen, feed her, and play with her. Kay took her mother shopping and we showed both of them the desert around Tucson. The visit lasted only ten days and after they had left, the house felt empty after this long flow of continuous visitors. But not for long, since two weeks after they left, Carmen and I took a flight to Germany.

My birth mother Edda around the time she met Ottie

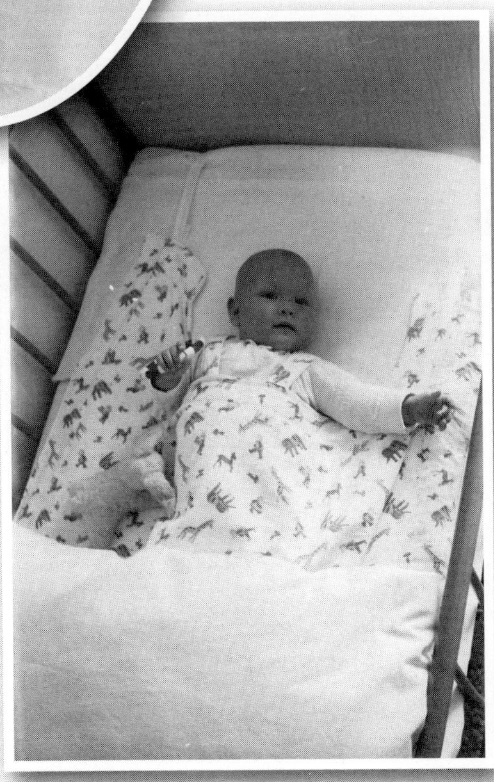

Me shortly after I was adopted in 1968

My mother Christiane and I, summer 1968

My father Karl Heinz and I after he came back from South America in the fall of 1968

My brother Christopher and I in 1971, Germany

My father Karl Heinz with me and my brother in 1973, Germany

My parents in Tucson with me and Ross, February 1998

My home town: Market square Gau-Algesheim, Germany

My home town Gau-Algesheim, Germany

Second meeting with my birth mother Edda, summer 1998, Germany

Our daughter Carmen, November 2000, Tucson, Arizona

Carmen and Sean, 2002, Tucson, Arizona

My mother Christiane
with Sean,
Germany, 2004

My birth mother
Edda with Sean,
Germany, 2004

My mother
Christiane with
Carmen in
Tucson, 2004

Carmen and Sean in Tucson, 2004

My brother Christopher with Carmen and Sean, Grand Canyon, March 2004

Samantha, Matthew, Monte, Irene, Ross, Ottie, Julia, Carmen and Sean, Kentucky 2005

Monte, Sam, Julia and Matthew with our Grandfather Ottie Garrett Sr.

Carmen and Sean in Belvidere, Illinois

Ross, me, Carmen and Sean in Illinois

My mother, me, Carmen and Sean in Madison, Wisconsin

Irene dressing up Carmen and Sean as Amish, Oregon, Wisconsin

Irene and I in Heidelberg, Germany, 2007

Irene and my mother Christiane in 2007, Germany

Me, Edda and her sister Editha in 2007, Germany

My brother Christopher and I, summer 2010, Germany

My birth mother Edda with Carmen and Sean, summer 2010, Germany

My birth mother Edda and I, summer 2010, Germany

CHAPTER 11

All My Families

We decided to let Carmen be baptized in the church in my hometown where we married. Ross was to come two weeks after us, since he did not have much vacation. Carmen and I flew at the beginning of December 2000, so we could meet with my friends and family, and he was to follow two days before the baptism in the middle of December. Christopher and Heike would be the godparents. Our plan was to fly back together right after Christmas and to stop in Illinois to visit Ross's family and celebrate a second Christmas there.

The flight to Germany with an eight month old was very strenuous. In addition, the time change disrupted Carmen's sleep pattern even more than usual, and I was soon completely deprived of sleep. Edda kept asking if I could find the time to meet with her and my sisters. The eight-hour trip to northern Germany where they lived seemed to me an impossible task during the short time we had in Germany before Ross was coming, especially with a baby, which had decided not to sleep for more than a maximum of two hours at a time, night or day. In addition, traveling by train with an infant seemed a horrific idea. To Edda's dismay, I decided not to see her this time. At least, I thought, she had been to Tucson just recently. My sister Christine, on the other hand, had just recently moved to Frankfurt and I could drive there with my mother's car in a little less than an hour. Christine was, therefore, the only one of my birth family whom I met that Christmas time. Christine and I met at the university cafeteria and had lunch together. I brought Carmen and we took a cute picture of Christine with Carmen. We only spent a short time together, since Christine had to work and Carmen had to go back home and sleep, maybe. I was glad to at least see Christine, since I liked her very much. Since we both tend to live in various countries it is very difficult to find a place and time to meet.

This time traveling in Germany was stressful for me, and the lack of sleep was really getting to me. On top of it all, Ross called and informed me that his grandmother's condition worsened and she had been hospitalized. Ross had a very special relationship to his grandmother and did not want her to die without seeing her at least once more. He was thinking about not coming to Germany, but instead staying in Illinois, if her condition did not improve. I was terrified. This was Carmen's baptism and I wanted him there; but I could understand his feelings and his grandmother was more important.

Despite all, Carmen was the one who had a great time in Germany. She loved getting all the attention of my mother and brother; I did not know how she could be so happy, seemingly without sleep. I was very grateful when Ross decided to come to Germany after all, since his mother told him that his grandmother was doing better. The baptism was a nice ceremony, small and family-oriented. My three aunts, my cousin, my father's two cousins, Heike, Stefan, and Bärbel and her family were there, and of course my mother and Christopher. After the ceremony, we went to a local restaurant to have lunch. Then we went home to, guess what, have coffee and cake.

Christmas in Germany is a very special time for me. You may know that in Germany the "Christkind" (Christchild) brings the presents on the evening of the twenty-fourth of December. In our family, on December 25, right after church, our family would drive to my aunt's house and have a Christmas party there. I love this tradition, since all my aunts and cousins would be there. My aunt makes the best turkey you can imagine. It was a tradition that had started through my Uncle Jimmie from California, when he was still living in Germany. His tradition of making turkey on Christmas had continued for over thirty years! My aunt would make "Knoedel," potato dumplings with it, and the best stuffing you can imagine. My cousin, Andrea, and her husband were also able to come from Madison, Wisconsin, and it would be the first and last Christmas in years where we all were together. The pictures I took with Carmen sitting in front of the Christmas tree reminded me of my own childhood. She looked so much like me with her absence of hair, her chubby cheeks and legs. I was in Heaven so to speak. As it was the twenty-seventh of December already, we left for Chicago.

It was a sad time. Ross's grandmother died on January 1st, her 85th birthday. It was a sad, yet not unexpected death. The funeral was set and we were able to be there before we had to go back to Tucson. Lots of people came, and Carmen was just very excited about all the flowers and people. I think having an innocent baby at a funeral somehow loosens the tightness of the event, and Kay and Ross's brother Grant seemed to be relieved that Carmen was there to deflect their attention. Louise had raised her daughter as a single mother, and now, after I was a mother myself, I could really comprehend what that meant. Although I applaud all the women who do a fantastic job of raising their children without a partner, I am very grateful that Edda had decided to give me up for an adoption. I guess a big part in this is who my parents are and the extremely good relationship I have with them. I cannot even envision other parents or having grown up differently. I hope that most adopted people who read this book have had a similar experience.

It was quite a contrast to come back home to Tucson. The pain of the loss of his beloved grandmother was hard on Ross. He always had a very special bond with his grandmother; she had been so down-to-earth, so natural, easy-going, and so grateful for life in general. The nice weather helped us a little to get our spirits back, and I decided to try to get back in touch with archaeology. I needed to continue studying if I ever wanted to finish my Ph.D. It was challenging for me though. I could spend hours just holding Carmen, watching her sleep, but I had the responsibility to finish my studies as well. So many people had helped me get that far, it seemed a shame to just give up. So I started preparing for my comprehensive exams, which was the next big obstacle in my life. Having no family at hand to help is really difficult for a young mother, especially when going to school. I wanted to quit badly, but just did not have the heart to do so. Edda wanted to help so much, and she told me that, if she was single, she would come and live with us and help. What a wonderful person, I would have loved to have her stay with us. Unfortunately, it also seemed to me that she was not happy with her life and her marriage and that made me sad. She could not just come and help me, he would always be with her and there was no way out.

I started to ask Edda more questions about Ottie. I really wanted to know more, but she reminded me that I could not write to her about this in the letters addressed to her. I needed to send those letters to one of my sisters. She told me that in all those years before I had contacted her, she thought about me every day, but never about him. He had left for apparently no reason. Edda knew he had siblings, but could not remember the name of his father. She told me that he was nine years younger than her. She understood that I wanted to know more about him and possibly meet him, but her husband could, under no circumstances, know about this. Thinking about all those events made Edda cry a lot, and my questions made her relive the whole terrible time all over again. She had been so hurt, so left alone. She was forced to give away what she had cherished most, her child, in order for me to have a better life; and, I suppose, she had really loved this man with all her heart. I started to think that maybe her husband did have a reason to be jealous. Ottie had been the first big love. Edda did not say this directly, but from the way she wrote about him, I got that distinct feeling.

When her pregnancy started to show, Edda moved in with her sister, far away from where her parents lived, so they would not know about her having a baby. Her parents were older at that time, and she did not want to burden them with her problems. The nursing home where she used to work, offered to raise me there while she was working, but Edda decided that this was not the right environment for a little child. I am not sure how I would have dealt with this situation. Edda's income was minimal, and she was afraid she did not have enough time and money to raise a baby the way it deserved. It must have been a tremendous decision to make up her mind on what to do. I know, one could say she should have kept me and used the opportunity to raise me in the nursing home. I do not completely share her opinion that this was not the right place, however, I am very happy I grew up with my parents and one can only really feel what someone else might have felt if one is in their shoes. You can hypothesize on what you would have done, but ultimately, nobody can. The only thing I know for sure is that Edda had an enormous inner struggle and did what she thought was best for me. And for this I am forever grateful to her. When Edda told me again how the nurse let her be alone with me for a while so she could hold me, I started crying. All that pain, all that suffering, and I could not give her that baby back.

I wrote to Edda that I was thinking about finding Ottie. She said that was okay, that is why she had kept the photograph and the address, but she would never want to hear from him again. Edda told me that when her husband is swimming she takes out the pictures of me and Carmen and looks at them in peace. As she had mentioned previously, she thinks a lot about what would have happened if Ottie had married her. She was proud that even Sophie, who usually did not display pictures, had photographs of Carmen in her apartment and at work. Christine and Amelie, too, had pictures of our family displayed in their apartments. Edda said that her husband was very surprised when he discovered this. I felt proud about that, but at the same time it scared me a little since it meant quite a responsibility. I had already learned that relationships are fragile in this family. After only one month being at daycare, Carmen came home one day and said "Kinder au." The word "Kinder" is German and means children and "au" I think is universal for pain. We never sent her back.

That summer we did not go to Germany, but instead visited Ross's family in Illinois. Carmen loved the farm, although there were no animals, but grass was new for her. In our garden in Tucson, there is no grass. Even though we have an 18,000-square-foot yard, there are only cacti, Palo Verde trees, mesquite trees, and gravel. Carmen was used to playing in the dirt and in the gravel. She barely wore shoes, but a child who is born in the desert, naturally adapts to the environment. She never got caught in the cacti, and knew not to touch the thorny trees and plants. She had never seen grass, and when her feet touched it the first time she was startled and kept playing next to the grass. It took her about two days to get used to the softness of the grass and even years later she kept telling me that grass was itchy!

In September 2001, I was finally ready for the comprehensive exam. The exam would take three weeks. I had five professors, each would give me one question and I had about ten pages for each question. I would start the countdown September twelfth. My mother booked a flight with American Airlines September tenth from Frankfurt to New York and then Phoenix, where I picked her up. That night, Carmen had terrible nightmares. She screamed almost the whole night, seemingly with no reason and nothing could make her stop. The next morning, on September eleventh, we got up exhausted and had the first breakfast with my mother. We do not watch TV, except sometimes in the evenings, and we do not listen to the radio in the morning, so we were completely unaware what had happened to the world. Suddenly, my cousin Andrea called from Wisconsin.

"Turn on the TV," she basically screamed into the telephone, "The Twin Towers are gone!"

We turned on the TV and were stunned. It seemed like a bad dream, like this could not be true. My mother had just come from there with American Airlines the day before. How could life ever be the same? I kept seeing the images of people jumping out the windows to end their suffering. It was like the tarot card of the falling tower. How could this be true?

The next day I got the questions for my comprehensive exam. It was so difficult to concentrate on this exam; everything seemed so meaningless after what had happened in the world. We had friends in New York at that time, but thank goodness they were not hurt. I prayed for all the families who had been affected in one way or another by those events. I think everybody in the world somehow had a connection with New York, either through a prior visit, business relations, friends, or family. Every time I closed my eyes, I saw the towers fall like a movie that never stops. But somehow I managed to finish. It was not the good result I had hoped for, but my committee was kind and they gave me six more months to prepare, to finally do the oral part of this exam. Then I would be a Ph.D. candidate and could start to work on my dissertation. What in the world was I thinking? I had to work quite a bit! Each of the five professors gave me special assignments in order to prepare. During the time I worked on the oral exam something else happened that would change our life as a family. Ross and I had decided that now was the time to think about a second child. It seemed though that thinking about it was already enough for me to get pregnant. I did not want to tell my committee of this change, because I did not want them to just let me pass because I was pregnant. I seem to never really gain that much weight and like to wear wide dresses, so I could hide it well. After I had passed my exam, which actually was easier than I thought, I told them the good news. I was then four months pregnant.

Edda was so proud to be a grandmother and so grateful that Carmen addressed her as that. Edda collected all the pictures from us, but she was so sad that she could not show them to anyone and tell the world what a happy grandmother she was. I felt so bad for her, but this was something she had to work out on her own. I do not feel betrayed having to tell her neighbor I am a family friend from a long time ago, but I feel bad for her. What I quite never understood is why she had so little say in this matter. This was her life too, and not just that of her husband. With all due respect, did she not have any say in their relationship? I do understand that thirty years ago, having an illegitimate child was not acceptable, but times have changed, and after all this suffering she should have a life of her own too.

As a treat for me and special surprise for my mother's birthday, I decided to fly to Germany with Carmen. Ross had to stay home, since he had to work. I figured that with two children it would be harder to travel, so better to go now. So when I was five months pregnant, Carmen and I flew to Germany. One special thing we would do this time in Germany was to finally bring my two families together. My mother had proposed that it was finally time to meet my birth family, and that included all of them. So my mother and I invited Edda, her husband, and all my three sisters to come to our house for lunch, and of course, coffee and cake. I was very nervous and had invited Heike as support.

My mother was surprisingly calm the day they arrived. I asked her about it and she told me that she knew that I was her daughter and nothing would change it. She would have had a hard time in the beginning, meeting my birth mother when my father had just died, but now she was emotionally stable and she was curious. She also knew how much it meant for Edda, with whom she had some telephone contact and had exchanged a few letters. My mother was excited to find out if I had inherited my character from my birth mother. She told me that she had been much more emotional the day I had met Edda for the first time, because she had been worried that I might be disappointed. In her view it was all about me, how I would feel and that I would be happy. She is just the most wonderful mother.

Then the car arrived at our house and I went downstairs to greet them. You have to walk up some stairs to get to our main door and my mother was waiting there to greet them. Edda and her husband were quite impressed by our big house and the incredible view, which oversees my picturesque hometown of Gau-Algesheim. We sat down in the living room to chat. Carmen, with her almost two-year innocence and her angel-like blond curls (yes, she finally got some hair, and beautiful hair too if I may say so) made the meeting less awkward. She just loved having people around and played with everybody with her little toy monkey. It is interesting you can buy just as many toys as you want, but when you get a free beanie baby in the shape of a monkey advertising some drug from the pharmaceutical industry, that will be the toy for life. Carmen would never leave without her monkey. She would wrap him with intense patience in a paper napkin, just to unwrap him later and then wrap him again. She was an angel in every sense of the word. She addressed my birth mother as Oma Edda, which made her so happy. Edda immensely enjoyed the brief time she had playing with Carmen downstairs without all the other people around. After a nice but simple lunch, Edda, her husband, and I went to the train station to pick up the three sisters. Heike came a little later and brought Carmen a very annoying duck game, which Carmen, of course, loved. Heike and Carmen have a special bond and I hope that it will always be that way. It was a good thing Heike was there. Later on, when my sisters left again, she entertained Edda's husband so that we had the chance to talk alone, at least for a little while.

When they all finally left I sat down and talked with my mother. She told me that she immediately liked Edda and that she felt confirmed that I had indeed inherited most of my characteristics from her. Without any jealousy, my mother pointed out all the similarities between my birth mother and me, and she seemed delighted. I could have not asked for a better outcome of this long-awaited meeting of my two families.

CHAPTER 12

Christmas in Germany

Tucson is hot in April, and when I came back the temperatures had already reached over one hundred. Being six months pregnant and with an almost two year old, bearing this heat is not easy. I was concerned about my blood pressure, so I took it easy this time. I somehow managed to work a little on my studies for the dissertation. This time we asked Ross's mother, Kay, if she would like to help us during the time around birth. I think she was really honored that we chose her and not my mother this time. I wanted her to feel that she was just as much part of this family as my mother. Kay planned to come for at least four weeks, starting two weeks before the due date, just in case.

I think Edda really wanted to come too, but her husband would not let her visit on her own and it would be too much for us to have both of them come for one month. In addition, Karl really did not want to fly anymore. Edda, though, missed me, and my little family. Since the day I was born there had never been even one day she did not think about me.

I called Edda from time to time, but unfortunately we both could not speak freely when Karl was around. This time I had questions about her pregnancy with me. I was considering a planned Cesarean birth for the baby whose gender we did not know yet, and I wanted to hear her advice. After all, this is a topic I unfortunately could not discuss with my mother, since she never experienced giving birth. Edda talked about the birth of my three sisters, as her husband was listening in on our conversation. As soon as she hung up the phone though, she wrote a letter telling me all about my birth. While she wrote, she also recalled the time shortly after I was born. She had sneaked into the baby unit of the hospital where I was born, and one of the nurses would allow her to hold me. Holding me in her arms, she had sworn to give me parents, both a father and a mother, and she had stood to her promise. The fear of not knowing if my parents were really good to me and if I was happy had, over the years, filled her heart with fear and pain. She was so endlessly relieved to finally hear how wonderful my parents were. Edda was deeply moved by my mother telling her how grateful my parents had been for her to give them the long awaited baby girl.

Edda's deepest wish was that Ross and I would move closer to Germany, so that we could join the family gatherings. I myself had started wanting to move back to Germany. I think when you have children of your own, you tend to want to live where you grew up, so they can have the same experiences you had as a child. But who knows what the future would bring? Being a Southwestern archaeologist is not as useful in Germany as one might think, and Ross did not speak German well enough to apply for jobs in Germany. His German improved constantly though, since he was successfully taking classes for two semesters.

Then, shortly before my due date, Ross and I made a new discovery. For my birthday, Ross promised to do more research on Ottie. He discovered using birth and death records that Ottie's parents were divorced and his mother had passed away. Ottie had one brother and one sister. And Ross made another stunning discovery. A woman by the name of Ruth Irene Garrett had published a book called *Crossing Over*. It was about her life growing up Amish, and how she had to leave the Amish community because she fell in love with a man who was not Amish. The man she fell in love with was Ottie Garrett, my birth father! We immediately ordered the book. It was shipped a few days later, but by this time I was so nervous about the birth I could not even think about reading it. The due date had come, and the baby was not there yet! Carmen was three weeks early, so I had never been in that phase where you just cannot wait any longer for the baby to arrive. In addition, the baby stopped moving and I got scared. I had nightmares and when I went to my gynecologist the next day, I told her about them. My doctor was absolutely fantastic, understanding, and incredibly supportive. She told me that there was no medical reason not to push it a little, and that the following day, Saturday the tenth of August, on my late father's birthday, we would induce the birth! I was so relieved. Kay was already there and I knew Carmen would have so much fun with Grandma that she would not even miss Ross and me.

Ross and I packed our bag; it included clothing for me and the baby, also some *Friends* videos and Irene's book. We also packed a little doll family, which the baby would bring for Carmen as a present. I was hoping that Carmen would not get jealous of the newborn baby, and to make it a little more appealing it would bring her a present. I also thought that, giving her a doll family, a mama, a daddy, a little girl, and a baby would give her the chance to play out her own experiences with the new family situation. I was hoping that if she had problems I would recognize it in her play.

Nothing happened for a long time, and Ross and I walked through the whole hospital with my IV in pursuit. Two hours after the water was broken, still nothing happened. Ross started reading Irene's book to me. We did not get very far, but we did learn that she was not Ottie's first wife, but that there had been several others before her. We also learned that my birth father had six children from these marriages! We were interrupted in our reading adventure when the decision was made to give me petosin, a labor-inducing medication. Oh boy, then things started to move forward! I was not in the mood for family history anymore, but wanted to watch *Friends*, my all-time favorite TV show, instead. I laughed so hard, that I swear I finally really relaxed, and two hours and four episodes later, Sean was born. Sean was born exactly on the day of my late father's seventy-sixth birthday. It was very emotional, and I cried for a long time, because he would never see his grandchildren who he had longed for so deeply.

The next morning, Ross brought Kay and Carmen to the hospital to introduce Carmen to her new baby brother. Carmen was delighted to see him and she loved the dolls we pretended that Sean brought for her. Carmen had fun with Grandma and in one day I would come back home, and that was all there was. We gave Irene's book to Kay to read since I probably would not have much time to read for the next few weeks. Carmen was a good big sister. She would sit on the couch and I put the "Boppy" around her and placed little Sean on it. She would sit totally still and watch her little brother, especially with *Xaboomafoo* on TV.

Kay read Irene's book within one day. When she brought it back to me she said, "Nice photo of him and her."

Photo, what photo? I had not seen any photos. In my preoccupied mind I had not even realized that in the middle of the book there were photographs, and one was showing Ottie and Irene. Irene was a pretty woman and seemed really young, and he looked very likeable as well. I placed the small picture of him that Edda had given to me next to the photograph in the book to see if I could find any similarities. After all, I was not completely sure if he was really my birth father. I kind of thought so, since there had been only two Ottie Garretts in the U.S. However, I would have to verify two facts before I could be really sure: Was his middle initial "A" and had he been stationed in Germany in 1967? In the photograph in the book he was no longer blond, his hair had darkened. But as a matter of fact so had mine, after Carmen was born. Irene described in her book that due to an accident, and being locked to a wheelchair as a result, Ottie had gained quite a bit of weight, but he was a very attractive man nevertheless. Actually, Irene wrote so nicely and lovingly about him that all my negative feelings for him melted away. I realized at that moment that the time to contact him had finally come.

When we saw Sean the first time, it seemed as if I had seen

him before. Yes, there was no doubt, even Ross noticed, Sean looked like ... yes, like Ottie! That small picture of an eighteen-year-old soldier had exceptional similarity to this little newborn baby! Even my mother noticed the similarity from a photograph we sent via email, without us hinting at it. She immediately told Edda, who also agreed!

Having helping hands for the time after a birth is a wonderful thing. You can sleep while someone watches the baby and the toddler. Kay, the baby, and Carmen got along famously, and the recovery from this birth was so much faster than from the one with Carmen. After only a week I could take Kay out with the car and do some minor shopping by myself. Both my mother and Edda were so happy that we were all healthy and that the birth had been so much easier this time. My sisters were all really excited as well, and could not wait to receive the first pictures. It seemed our relationship had gone back to normal and I really wanted them to be the aunts of our two children.

In October, two months after Sean's birth, my mother came to meet her new grandson, and of course, see if her daughter was fine. A mother does never cease to be your mother. You can be fifty and a grandmother yourself and I am sure your mother will treat you like a child, will care for you, as if you were still a baby. Well, at least mine will, that is for sure. It is a very emotional moment when you present a new grandchild to your mother for the first time. My mother started crying and that of course made me cry too. I wished so much that I could be closer to home, so my mother could participate more in the children's lives. It is so difficult to be so far away from your family. I wanted to be a good mother and I could appreciate all my mother did for us even more now, since I was one myself.

This time my mother and I did not go to California. My Uncle Jimmie had passed away a few months before Sean was born, and my aunt was terminally suffering from cancer. My aunt, during my pregnancy, had envisioned a boy with red hair. When Sean was born I called her and told her that it was indeed a boy with blond hair and a tint of red. Shortly after his birth, her mind could not focus anymore, and a few weeks after my mother visited my aunt died. I was very upset because she had been like another mother to me, even though she also lived far away and our relationship had not always been the best, but it had developed through time and I had grown to love her in a very special way. It was like losing a mother.

It was mid-January 2003, on a Saturday morning. Ross, our two young children, and I were sitting in our white minivan on the way from Tucson to Phoenix. Sean was only five months old and this would be his first flight. I was taking him on this 1.5 hour flight to Modesto, California. It was a sad occasion. We were flying to the memorial service for my aunt and uncle. Originally, I had not planned on being at the memorial service. Sean was still so little and Carmen was not even three yet. My mother and her youngest sister Gaby had come for the service. I talked to my aunt on her deathbed and that was more important than being at a service I told myself. But then, when I talked to my mother on the phone and she described the empty house where my aunt and uncle had spent their last 32 years, I started crying. I was supposed to be there, I had been her favorite niece and I had close contact with her for the last six years. My mother had seen her for the first time in 30 years only two years before because of me, and Aunt Gaby had not seen her sister since she had left Germany in 1971. I was the one who was supposed to be there. I was almost hysterical and my mother started comforting me. She understood my pain and told me she would buy me a ticket to come the short trip from Arizona to California, if I wished to do so.

I did. My cousin, one of Aunt Maria's two sons, would fly from Minnesota to Modesto, the same day as Sean and I. He would wait there for me, to take us and his son, Shane, to Sonora. Ross would stay home with our daughter Carmen. Everything seemed to be planned perfectly. Ross and Carmen said their goodbyes at the Phoenix Airport and I boarded the plane. It left right on time. A woman, a little younger than me, sat next to me. She had blond shoulder-length hair and a nice smile. She seemed not to mind Sean. Behind us though, sat a woman who was obviously annoyed by having a baby so close to her. Well, it would only be 90 minutes and I was there. Sean cried a little when we took off and the woman behind us recommended giving him Benadryl to calm him down. I am not giving a baby Benadryl for any reason. I was a little upset, but the nice woman next to me comforted me. She seemed to be really taken by Sean and we started talking.

Soon we were approaching Modesto, when things started to change. There was a thick fog and the pilot informed us that at this moment it was impossible to land. We would be circling around for a while to see if the weather would allow the landing. The short circling turned into an hour, and then two. Sean was hungry and so was I. There is no food on a short flight like this, but I was nursing and started feeling quite hungry. Fortunately, I was nursing Sean. I also started getting worried about diapers, since I had only packed two on the carry-on, the rest were in the suitcase, which was not accessible to me. A couple sitting a few rows back suddenly came to me and asked if I wanted a banana that the woman had in her purse. She saw me nursing and knew I needed food to keep the milk supply ready. I accepted gratefully. Sean was incredibly quiet considering he was in this tiny space with loud noises of the engines.

My neighbor and I warmed up to each other and I somehow mentioned that I was adopted and recently found my birth mother. Something changed in Amy when she heard me say this and she shared that several years prior she placed for adoption her five-month-old baby girl. The baby was the same age as Sean was then. I felt a deep empathy for this young woman. She told me she missed her baby very much, but she was using drugs at the time, and living in a cold abandoned house. One day, when the baby was five months old, she suddenly had an awakening moment, realizing she could not raise a baby like this, so she placed her up for adoption. It was an open adoption and she would visit the little girl sometimes, being introduced as a distant relative. My heart opened for this woman. I told her about my birth mother and her pain of giving me away since she had no partner and no paying job and she was helpless. She wanted me to have a good, safe home, with a father and a mother. When I met her seven years earlier, being already twenty-nine years old, she told me that there had not even been one single day without thinking about me, even though she had married and had three more daughters. Oh, how much I could feel for Amy who had just done what she knew was best for her baby, but how much she missed her.

The plane suddenly sped up, its nose went up, and we sped away. The fuel was running out and we had to fly to Oakland to land. The plane just made it. There we stood in the middle of the runway and had to be picked up by buses because the plane was out of fuel. Now, a whole airplane full of people was waiting at the Oakland Airport, where nobody wanted to be. We waited for two more hours until the airline sent three big buses to bring us all to the Modesto Airport by road. Waiting at the airport, all the people in the plane started to talk to each other. Magically, probably because we were, after all, in the "same boat," all anger and frustration subsided. The woman, who in the beginning complained about Sean, told me now what a good baby he had been. Other people were exchanging phone numbers and cell phones to call their loved ones to tell them we were fine, just late. People I had never seen before helped me get food and diapers. Amy and I took the same bus, as did the lady who would still sit behind us. Stories circled about what people had planned to do that day. One woman missed her father's funeral, another the first day of an important conference. But somehow this no longer seemed important. The whole airplane crowd became like a family. It was a most happy crowd. I called Thomas who was still waiting at the airport, telling him when I would arrive. When we passed the Golden Gate Bridge, the fog started to lift, the sun was setting, and I could see the Golden Gate Bridge and the Oakland Bay Bridge both together in the red-orange fog. It was the most amazing sight I have ever seen. I always carry a camera, but just then I could not find it in my big diaper bag. The image will be in my heart forever now.

We finally got to the airport in Modesto at 11 p.m., after a nine-hour-trip, what should have been only a ninety-minute flight. Everybody said good-bye. The lady behind us, whose name I never knew, looked at me and Amy standing together, not knowing exactly what to do or say.

"Now, would you just give each other a hug?"

We did. We exchanged addresses and parted. When I finally found my cousin and we were on our two-hour trip to Sonora, I started thinking about this trip. I had been upset and tired, but suddenly it occurred to me: I had done this trip and had to spend all of those hours in the airplane and the bus, just to meet Amy. It was all about her. Amy had to meet me, had to see that giving away her child had been a good thing. She had to meet me to hear that she would be fine, for me, as an adopted child, to tell her she did right. Some day, she and her husband would have their own baby and she would be a wonderful mother. I was sure about this. Unfortunately, I lost her address and we never met again. But I know in my heart that, just like me, she would never forget those nine hours we spent together, the bond we felt as an adoptee and a mother who had given her child up for adoption. When she had held Sean, she must have known that everything was fine, and that she should not feel guilt, but gratefulness, that her child was given a chance for a better life.

I also invited Edda to come and visit this year. She was not able to pay for the trip but was hopeful to see us next summer in Germany. I told her that Carmen had started saying her name. It sounded like "Adi" and Edda was incredibly proud. She said her heart filled with warmth when she read the letter in which I told her the news. Unfortunately, we could not afford a trip to Germany. It was just too expensive for all four of us, after all, Ross and I were both students, and he only had a part-time income. Edda told me in almost every letter that she was playing the lottery, so she could come and help us and pay a flight for us to come.

Then Kay, Grant, and Vargus came to celebrate Thanksgiving with us. It would become a tradition to celebrate my favorite holiday in our home. Christmas we would spend just the four of us, but with Kay and Grant and Vargus we did a little Christmas celebration the day after Thanksgiving. While other people fight for parking spots at the mall and try to get the best bargain on the biggest shopping day of the year, the Meyers family puts up the Christmas tree, decorates the house, and has a little pre-Christmas celebration.

Edda inquired curiously what I had found out about Ottie. I was to send my answer to Amelie. Edda mentioned again, that after she and Ottie were engaged, they met her parents, but it was an awkward and cold meeting. Edda's hypothesis was that her mother had felt at that point that something bad would happen. When the letter I wrote about Ottie arrived at Amelie's house, Edda started to worry. Amelie would not read it over the phone, but instead bring it during her next visit. Edda was curious and scared at the same time. Ottie played such a big role in her life, especially because of me, that news about him made her feel uneasy.

Karl though, was getting more used to me and my family. Although he still did not want anybody other than his daughters to know who I really was, he would talk about his friends in America and even remind Edda of my upcoming birthday and urge her to send my birthday card. Although I felt bad for Edda, that she could not openly present her grandchildren to anyone, I had started to actually really like her husband. Edda was always so grateful that he liked me and even cared about my family. I think his position was actually not very easy. I do think that he had a real reason to be afraid that Edda would prefer me over their daughters or at least not pay as much attention to them. And after all, that was his and her family and they were the most important parts of his life.

Finally, Edda was able to read the letter I wrote about Ottie.

She was touched by the way I had written the letter, telling her that she was most likely so much better off with her husband, considering that Ottie had been married and divorced several times, with children from different marriages. Most likely she would have been divorced in a foreign country and then would have been a single mother. It was better this way, I was sure of it. I am not sure though, if that would console a woman who loved a man, had born his child, and had gone through so much hardship. Did she ever think that maybe he would have not been divorced if he had married her? I do not know, but I could imagine her feeling like this. Edda was so happy that I obviously inherited so much from her family. She was sad that I would never meet her brother, whom she loved so much, but maybe some day I would be able to meet her sister. She did not know then that it would take another five years until I met her, and that the circumstances were much stranger than either one of us could have imagined.

In February, we had a big party. It was Sean's baptism. This time, due to lack of money and because my cousin Andrea would be one of the godparents, we would have the baptism in Tucson and not in Germany. My brother came to visit, and then my cousin, Henning, the other godparent. My brother and Henning overlapped for one week, and then Christopher left and Henning stayed. My cousin Andrea and her husband came from Madison, Wisconsin, and my cousin Thomas and his wife, Candia, from Minnesota. Thomas is Aunt Maria's youngest son. We met when I was in my early 20s and over the years, and after his parents died, his brother Steven and I were basically his only relatives. We had developed an almost sibling-like relationship, which was caring and loving. We would call each other about once a week, just as his mother and I had done. His wife, Candia Lee Cole, is an eco-mentor with honorable intentions to save this world and its inhabitants. Thomas is a devoted husband, who loves his wife more than anything on earth. Being with them I am filled with peace and interesting conversation.

Kay did not come, since she had just been there, and there were so many people, and she was not Catholic. A new deacon, who had just come to Tucson from his native county of Mexico, very nicely performed the Mass. His English was not so great yet, but he was the most enthusiastic person about his devotion you could meet. Henning loves computers, and he made a beautiful CD with all the pictures of the baptism, which I sent to Edda. Sophie was able to show it to her parents on the computer. Oh, how I love modern technology. Just some years ago, this would have been impossible.

Life went on in hot Tucson. During the summer we went on our first camping trip with a family of four. I had to do some final research for my dissertation and so we decided to make it a family trip. Our first stop was Mesa Verde in Colorado. Mesa Verde, Spanish for green table, is the nation's richest archaeological preserve with over 4,000 prehistoric sites, including 600 cliff dwellings. In December 1888, a Colorado rancher named Richard Wetherill was looking for stray cattle at the mesa top, when he saw a cliff dwelling in the side of Mancos Canyon. At first glance the dwelling looked as if it was still inhabited, which it was not. The site was later called Cliff Palace.

Ross and I bought a big, three-room tent, and were planning on doing our first camping trip with children. Blessed are the inventors of the minivan. We packed a baby travel bed, a table and chairs, a huge mattress, our comfy sheets, toys, diapers, cooking pots, dishes, a grill, and all kinds of other things one might or might not need on a family camping trip. The campsite was marvelous, the area was wooded and the campsites located within the natural environment without changing its ambient of nature. Being at an elevation of 8,500 feet, the nights were much colder than we had anticipated. The kids, though, were great and they enjoyed the climbs to the individual cliff dwellings. Ross would carry Carmen and I had the "Kelti Kit," which Christopher had bought two years prior for Carmen, to carry the almost thirty-pound Sean up the ladders of the cliff walls and into the sites. It was not quite as easy as

I let people believe, but after a few older people had admired my strength and endurance I could not do anything other than pretend it was easy. I took the most amazing photographs of the picturesque cliff dwellings, with their 800-year-old brick walls, the pictographs, doorways leading into a past life of the ancient Pueblo people. I could have stayed there forever, but we had little children, and as you might guess, that did not work.

At home a letter from Edda awaited me. She was already so excited that we were planning on coming to Germany for Christmas. I had written to her about our plans this year, and that we were definitely planning on visiting them in their home this time. I think Edda already knew all the meals she would cook for us in December, although it was only the end of July at this time. She and her husband already planned everything, they would be giving us their bedroom and they would sleep in a neighbor's house. My sisters also planned on coming to their parent's house while we were visiting. But this was still four months in the future.

Edda's letters still kept coming in regular sequences, but they were less emotional now. That was not a bad thing, I think it meant that our relationship had reached a point where we were more secure about each other, we had covered almost all past events and possible questions about those times, we had lived through a time when our relationship was threatened by the outside world and the reaction of both our families, it was now time to relax and just be ourselves. Her letters contained more information about daily events and what my sisters were doing, as they and I did not write each other that often. After finishing her Masters degree, Christine had started another university program, and Sophie had moved to a nice apartment with a roof terrace closer to her work. All three seemed to be doing fine. Edda was still planning our trip to their house and I think the simple prospect of us coming made her happy. My sisters would be arriving one day after our arrival and we would all be spending two days together. On the fourth day,

Ross, myself, and the children would leave. I still do not know what identity we were given to the neighbors Edda and Karl were staying with, but it also did not really matter to me. Karl still did not want anybody to know about me; but he bought the train tickets for our visit and that was really generous of him. I think he was in a real dilemma, on the one hand, he really liked Ross and me, and the kids, and in a way he felt like a grandfather to them. On the other hand, he could just not risk people talking badly about Edda and her child out-of-wedlock.

I emailed Sophie about our upcoming visit, but she did not answer. Edda felt it necessary to apologize for her. She told me that lately, Sophie's health was not as good and that her job was hard and her colleagues were not nice to her. She had trouble walking up the stairs to her new apartment because of her rheumatism, and was just not herself lately. I felt bad for Sophie, I really liked her a lot and I was hoping that we could become friends some day, real friends. But I guess good things take a while.

Mid-December of 2003, Ross, the kids, and I flew together to Germany. Flying with two small children by myself just did not seem doable at that time. Sean was now sixteen months old and Carmen almost four years old. For Carmen, this trip was essential for her development, especially for her speech. Until this trip she spoke a mixture of English and German, and although I was sure that she spoke German just fine, she was afraid to do so at first. During the first week in Germany she did not even say one word in German. In the second week however, something changed and suddenly, from that moment on, my little baby girl was truly bilingual! Out of the blue she understood that German and English were two separate languages and that they could be used independently of one another.

Sean, though, was just very excited about the trains in Germany, used not only to travel greater distances but also to go shopping in the neighboring town. We, for example, took the train to Mainz to the Christmas market and to northern Germany to visit Edda and her family. That particular trip was eight-hours long and we had to switch trains twice. The first train transfer was not too bad, but the second time we had to run from one side of the train station to the other… in two minutes… with two kids… and two suitcases, and that was not easy. But, we made it and got to the little train station of Edda's town safely. Karl was waiting at the train station and he had borrowed two car seats so we could drive to their tiny little town. It is beautiful up north, water canals run picturesquely along the streets, almost like in the Netherlands. The little villages have many red brick houses, and are adorned with lots of woodwork. The landscape is flat, but even though it was winter and the trees were bare one could imagine the beauty of this landscape with its flowers and trees and prairie-like landscaping. I had never been that far north in Germany and really immensely enjoyed the peacefulness of this region.

Edda was anxiously awaiting our arrival. The kids absolutely adored her and they were soon very close. Carmen and Sean really took to Karl, as well, and he played with them endlessly and with a great devotion. Edda had baked several cakes, and before it was dinnertime we had the obligatory coffee and cake. Then we settled in a little, and talked a very long time. Edda prepared a wonderful dinner for us with baked fish. She is an excellent cook, and I would really like to learn cooking from her. We slept, as was planned for months, in their bedroom. The kids were fine, and although Edda had organized a kids' crib for Sean, all four of us ended up in their huge king-size bed. It was then that Ross and I decided to finally spend the money and buy a king-size bed ourselves. You can read all about how to make your child sleep in their own bed, but when it comes down to it, they end up in your bed anyway. After all, it is you who needs enough sleep as well. We had a very nice queen-sized bed, but it ended up that when both kids would come over, which was 80 percent of the nights, Ross would end up on what we called "Papa's bed," a mattress stored in front of the queen bed, ready with sheets, which just had to be pulled out so Ross could sleep on it when our bed was too crowded. We decided in Edda's bed that "Papa's bed" would finally retire and we would buy a king-size bed ourselves.

The next day we had breakfast with homemade bread and fresh milk from the farm. What a treat! Then we went for a small walk through the neighborhood and the playground. It was getting cold and it looked like snow. In the afternoon the "girls" arrived. They were really happy to see us, but Sophie was not feeling so well and she kept her distance. I was used to that now, and learned to not take it personally. Who was I to judge someone who was in constant pain? I was sincerely hoping though, that some day, she could find something to help her ease her suffering. Ross gave Sophie some advice on a dietary supplement he had heard of, and she actually started taking it. Carmen though, who did not know any of this, suddenly took Sophie's hand and asked,

"Does this hurt? You will feel better soon."

Sophie was stunned, but for some reason believed in the honesty of this little innocent child.

In the afternoon, as expected, it started snowing. We had to stay inside the house, something Ross did not like so much, since he is claustrophobic. Their house is rather small, and Ross told me later he had the feeling he was locked inside a closet for four days. The kids, though, had fun with all those people. They started cleaning Edda's sliding door with a loving devotion, and to this day Edda talks about all the little handprints she did not want to clean for weeks after we had left, as a memory to her little adorable grandchildren.

We had coffee and cake first – please believe me, Germans really do have that much coffee and cake, it is a customary social event – and later another one of Edda's wonderful dinners. According to Ross we ate so much he had the feeling that this was all we did while we were visiting them. Every time a meal was over, the table was immediately set for the next delight. It was all delicious, though. On the third morning, we went for a walk in the snow and then let the kids play in the snow-covered yard. They loved it, and we took some beautiful photographs of them and my sisters. Of course, as I realized later, we did not take all the pictures we should have. Have you ever realized that the pictures you later want the most, you never took? In this case, we did not take a photograph of me and my birth mother together, or Edda with both kids, or one with all of us together. I realized that you take the least number of photographs of the most important people or your best friends. They were always there so I never took pictures, but when somebody comes to visit who is usually not there, you take many pictures. Anyway, we had a great time but we were also excited to get back home and celebrate Christmas. Sean was so excited during the train trip home I think he constantly moved the entire eight hours! I was really glad we visited Edda and her family up north. This had been a wonderful, warm experience for all of us, and especially for the kids to get more familiar with this side of my growing family. I think even Karl realized that, although I did not want the kids to call him "Opa Karl," he was part of the family and the kids like him very much.

The rest of our stay in Germany went fast. We had a peaceful Christmas with my mother and brother on Christmas Eve and a family Christmas at my aunt's house on the twenty-fifth, as we have done for thirty years. A few days after New Years it was time to fly back home. I did not know that what followed would be the longest time I would spend away from Germany. I also did not know that the following Christmas we would spend with a family that I, at this point in time, did not even know I had.

CHAPTER 13

Kentucky Relations

Tucson, in the winter, is a nice place to be. The weather in January is sunny and warm and you cannot even imagine it being cold and snowy some place else. My cousin, Thomas, would call from time to time and inquire about the weather. Living in St. Paul, Minnesota, his dream was to live in a sunnier region, and he was dreaming about being outside and hiking with us. After the grey, rainy Germany, we could appreciate the mild Tucson winter once more in its full extent. This is the time to hike and be outside, and the memories from Germany had started to fade again. We were back home, back with our friends, our daily life. Edda, on the other hand, was re-living the memory of our visit in its fullest. Her next few letters were full of fond memories of our visit to her home. I could feel her happiness and her relief that the visit had passed so peacefully. She was just a little sad that she could not tell anyone about her beautiful and loving grandchildren, and how happy she was to be a grandmother. I cannot even imagine having to keep a secret like this. Personally, I love to talk, sometimes a little too much. I tend to get very excited about everything, and I like to share my experiences and emotions with my friends and family. Sometimes that is not the best thing to do, but on the other hand, I do not have secrets from anybody.

Our successful visit to Edda's home had initiated another event. Amelie and Sophie were planning on visiting us in Tucson for three weeks. Six weeks after we had come back from Germany, the two of them arrived. The kids were very excited, and they went with me to pick their aunts up at the airport in Tucson. The kids remembered them well, and thus they were not shy at all, and that made Sophie really happy. She was still a little apprehensive towards me, but being together for three weeks made a big difference. Amelie and Sophie loved our guesthouse, where they had their own little apartment. They both very much enjoyed being with the children, and I had time to take them to places.

I especially enjoyed going out, with just the two of them, at night twice. Ross watched the kids so the three of us could go to one of my favorite coffee shops and get to know each other better without being distracted by the kids. The coffee shop we went to is called Epic Café, and is located close to the university on the corner of Fourth Avenue and University Street. It is a fun place, with liberal arts and advertisements and little tables along the windows. The food is delicious, and I absolutely love their chocolate mousse, which comes in little tiny espresso cups. But boy, when you eat them, you can barely even finish one of those tiny cups. Even for a chocolate lover like me, this is almost too dense. But the taste is absolutely heavenly! I also like the ambience of students studying or artists performing their newest compositions. I have very fond memories of the three of us going there and talking about us, our relationship, and our future.

Amelie is an open person, as I am, and is not afraid of talking or exposing her feelings and thoughts, while Sophie is more reserved and it is more difficult to get to know her. It is too bad, since I really, really like her. I would like for her to trust me, but I know it will take a long time and maybe it will never happen. We live so far apart and to get to know each other requires a lot of trust, and that is something she does not really have in general. I wonder why this is.

I felt though, that we made a lot of progress in our relationship, and I was kind of sad when they left. I knew that, over time, the closeness we started to feel would subside and the next time we would meet, we would have to work on our relationship once again. It is strange, meeting my sisters. I just wished I would have met them earlier, and we could have been real sisters, something I think might never happen. But I am glad to at least know them now, and hope we can become friends.

One thing we started discussing while they were there was Ottie. I told them I knew his address and was thinking about writing him, but that I felt bad because of our mother. I did not want to hurt her. Both my sisters were too curious themselves, and they actually begged me to contact him, so they, too, could know who he was. I guess, they were really curious who their mother was in love with so long ago. Maybe, for them, it meant to get to know their mother better. I was amused by their devotion for me to write and send this letter, but it meant we had to kind of lie to our mother, well, at least not tell the truth. I was planning on contacting him first, and then, depending on his reaction, eventually telling Edda. I was really scared how Edda would react, since she had written to me that she would give me his picture, but he did not deserve me and that he was dead to her. I really wanted to know who he was, though. After all, he was part of me, just as much as she was. Through his wife Irene's book I had also learned he was very overweight, and it was possible, although I did not really want to think so, that he would not live to be very old, and this was the time to contact him.

I started composing a letter to him, and gave it to Amelie and Sophie to read and comment on. They approved of it and supported my wish to send the letter. Everything was ready, the letter written, but I could just not decide if I should send it or not. I was a little afraid. This was different than contacting Edda. I knew that she had a sincere interest in knowing what happened to me through the letters to the adoption agency. But Ottie left, although he knew about me. Would he just not want me to be there? But his wife wrote so lovingly about him, and he had six other children, and he was only eighteen, so it was possible that he had changed. There is a big difference in being seventeen years old and being fifty-three years old. I was a little surprised by Amelie and Sophie's eagerness for me to contact him, since there were six more siblings who were also somehow involved in this. As it was, my three sisters were already competing for me and my attention, how would they feel about six more siblings to compete with? They had not thought about this, and came to the conclusion that I should send the letter, get the answer, and then not continue the relationship. That was not possible, I told them. If I wrote this letter, just as with our mother, I would be responsible, and if Ottie wanted contact I could not just deny it. Just as I had to accept the fact, if he did not want to know me, I would have to accept him and his family just as I did Edda and her family. It was really difficult. When Amelie and Sophie left, I had still not decided what to do, but I did have their approval. And this is the letter I wrote:

Tucson, 10/20/2004

Dear Ottie A. Garrett,

I am not 100 % sure that you are the person I am trying to find. If this is you on this picture in about 1967 in Gersfeld, Germany, then this letter is for you. If not, which I do not think, then please let me know.

I was born January 29, 1968 in Germany and my mother Edda gave me the name Christine. I know you must think I am a boy because she had written this to you. She only did this as a last attempt, hoping you would come back. She knew that you wanted a boy.

When I was three months old my birth mother finally reached the hard decision to give me for adoption so I would have a mother and father to raise me. I have wonderful parents and a brother. My parents changed my name to Julia Isabell. I met Edda nine years ago. She had married two years after I was born and has three daughters with her husband. They are a great family and we write and visit each other from time to time. She had saved this picture of you for me including your military address at that time.

I studied Anthropology in Frankfurt, Germany and received my

M.A. in 1995. In 1992 my professor had sent me to Arizona to participate in an excavation. It was then that I decided to become an archaeologist. I worked in the US, Germany, and Argentina. Since 1997 I am enrolled at the University of Arizona, working on my PhD. It is here where I met Ross and we got married in 1999. We have two children, Carmen is 4 and Sean is 2. Here is a picture of us this summer.

My husband and I found your name on the internet and I bought your book and later your wife's. I liked your book, since I am an anthropologist and I am very interested in other cultures and traditions. I liked Irene's book too, not just because she is your wife. Through these books I learned a lot about you and your family. However, I would like to learn more, especially about your children, including Philip.

I used to resent you, for leaving Edda and me. Now I do not feel this way anymore. I think everything happens for a reason, and I could not have wished for better parents and a better childhood.

If you would like to learn more about me, you are welcome to ask. I for myself would just like to have closure and learn a little more about where I came from. I hope this letter does not disturb you and your family, this is really not my intention. I just suddenly felt I should write to you and tell you who I am and that I do not feel any anger towards you. I hope you and Irene will be happy. She seems to be a very special person.

Sincerely,
Julia I. Meyers

It took me several months to actually send the letter. I remember that it was already fall, well, in other parts it was already fall, in Tucson it was still midsummer and my mother was about to come for a visit. I remember exactly that it was a

Thursday morning, and I was on my way to the little local zoo with the kids, Ross was at work. I called him and he simply said,

"Do it."

So I decided it was time to send that already sealed and stamped letter. At that moment, I knew exactly that when I came back home from the zoo, the mail carrier would have been there and the letter would be gone. I put the letter in the mailbox, put up the flag, and left for the zoo. As expected, the letter was gone when I came back. Okay, it was in Ottie's hands now. I really did not expect anything, though. I was fine with whatever might happen. If he did not write back, that would be fine. But I would at least know that it was really him, and that he just did not want me to be in his life.

A week after I sent the letter, my mother came to visit from Germany. I was so happy that my mother came once a year for three to four weeks. It was very important to me that she played a big role in my children's lives, even though she lived so far away. I told my mother about the letter and showed her a copy of it. She liked the content and was almost as eager as I was awaiting Ottie's reply. Although my mother stayed for three weeks, nothing happened. No response. Towards the end of her visit, my mother asked carefully if I would be really upset if he never did contact me, or if I found out that he did not want to have contact with me ever. My dear mother always worried about me. I think as a mother, you just never stop worrying. I was her child and in her mind always in need of her protection. I could honestly tell her though, I would not be upset if Ottie did not reply. Most of all, I honestly, mainly wanted to know if it was him who Irene talked about in her book, and maybe a little bit more information about him. But if he decided not to want to be in contact, that was fine too, and I could live with that. After all, managing two sets of families (well, three including Ross's family) was already a lot.

My mother left on a Friday, and guess what? On Saturday morning, just as Ross and the kids left to do some errands, I found a letter in the mailbox. And the letter was from nobody else but Ottie! It was an interesting coincidence, it was just not meant to be there while my mother was still here, and I was supposed to receive this letter when I was completely alone, which really is a rare event when you have two small children. Then something very unexpected happened. I cried, I cried, and I cried. I could not stop crying and I had not even opened the letter yet! I do not know what came over me so suddenly. Maybe it had affected me much more than I had admitted to myself, maybe it did mean something to me after all, that he acknowledged he was my birth father. I went inside and looked at the letter for a long time. Then I opened it. Inside was a card with a bear in the snow and some birds on it and Ottie wrote:

Dear Julia,

Thank you so much for your letter, you have a beautiful family. Yes, the picture is of me when I was 18 and in the Army.

I was born Jan. 19, 1949 in Glasgow, Kentucky. I would love to write to you or even talk to you on the phone (your number is unlisted). Maybe someday, if you wish we can meet. I will answer any and all questions you have if you so wish. I am glad to hear your mother is happy.

Your husband is a fine looking young man and your children are as beautiful as their mother is. I am not much on writing so if you want to talk, call me. Irene and I travel a lot doing book signings and other types of speaking engagements across the Midwest, but we are home for the next several weeks.

Again thank you so much for writing,

Yours truly,
Ottie Garrett

Wow, I cried some more. Why in the world was I so emotional? I could not figure it out. It was almost as if I was relieved, as if a burden had been taken off my shoulders, a burden I never knew I carried. What a strange feeling of relief came over me. I had to call Heike and tell her everything. We always do that, but it is rare to actually reach her on the weekend. This time, as if she had known, she was there and I could tell her all my emotions and cry and laugh. By the time I could hear Ross and the kids drive into the gravel driveway, my tears had subsided. Ross realized immediately that something had happened and asked me. I showed him the letter.

"Well, there you go," was his response. I was just glad our phone number was unlisted. I could not have withstood getting a call without a warning. Can you image how emotional I would have been on the phone? I am a person who needs some time, as you might have figured out. I had to sleep over this first, and then in my own time, decide when I would call Ottie back.

The next day was Sunday, and I was very nervous. I could not wait any longer. I had to call. I wanted to do it alone, so while Ross played with the kids inside, I took my cell phone into the yard. With a racing heart, I called the number. I planned to work on my dissertation that weekend, but I can tell you that would not happen that weekend. I remember it like yesterday. It was warm and sunny, in mid-November. I was so nervous; I thought I might not be able to talk at all. But I still managed to somehow call.

He answered, "Hello," the way he always says hello with the emphasis on "e."

I answered, "This is Julia."

What a short, life-changing sentence. It was strange in the beginning, but his voice sounded so nice and he was so bubbly. Kind of like me, when I am nervous and I tell stories to compensate and to not allow a strange, uncomfortable silence in the conversation. He started telling me how Irene, his wife, had gotten the letter from the mailbox and given it to him. He had assumed it was fan mail for Irene and opened it. What he saw was the picture of himself as a young man, and he eagerly started reading. He could barely believe what the letter said. Irene saw his strange facial expression of disbelief and excitement, and asked what was wrong, so he told her just to read this letter. She immediately pointed out the similarities between Sean and him and Philip.

Philip was one of his two sons from his second wife. Philip died when he was just eighteen months old of sudden infant death syndrome. A few years later, Ottie and she divorced. She was now remarried. Monte had mainly grown up with his mother, but Ottie had a good relationship with him and he was very fond of his son.

I was so sad about Philip. I could still cry. I cannot imagine losing a child. And Monte, how must he feel; he had only been three years old. Suddenly, I remembered a strange memory. When I was about ten years old, I had created an imaginary older brother. I thought a long time about his name, and finally I had named him Philip. He was with me quite a long time and then after years, slowly disappeared. I wonder, was this a coincidence? Philip died when I was about ten years old, the exact same time I had created this imaginary brother.

After this, Ottie and I talked for a while about him and me, and we got a little more comfortable talking with each other. Finally, I addressed the question about why he left Edda, knowing that she was pregnant. He told me that he really loved her and that they were dating for about six months. They met on as many weekends as possible during this time, spending the whole weekend together, going out to eat, having picnics, and going hiking, which she loved. One time he even briefly met her father. The military told its young soldiers not to date German women, since the only thing they wanted was to become military wives and move to the U.S. Then one day, Ottie got the notice that he was sent overseas. He told Edda and she told him she was pregnant. They talked about getting married and how and where. Returning to the army base, Ottie immediately went to tell his chaplain about Edda and the baby. The chaplain's first response was that all women would say they were pregnant, which was probably a lie, because they wanted to move to America. He added that even if she was really pregnant, who would tell him that it was his?

Can you imagine such an atrocity? I so much want to tell this chaplain to his face what I think about him, really! Ottie was underage then, and therefore dependent on the military's permission. He never got a pass to leave the base again, and was sent back to the U.S. within the next few weeks. He could not write Edda, since he did not have her address. And being eighteen, he figured that the chaplain was probably right. It was just easier to accept this version. Poor Edda, can you imagine being her during this time? I cannot even imagine the pain she must have gone through. I almost felt guilty. Here I was, having a great life, having the opportunity of having two fathers and two mothers, while she could not even tell anybody that she found me, that she was a grandmother. Her pain just never seemed to end.

Ottie then told me about his other six children, my siblings. I have five brothers, including Philip, and one sister. Unfortunately, Ottie does not have contact with two of my brothers. Those children are from previous marriages with the common agreement not to share custody. The other three children partially grew up with Ottie. There is Monte, Philip's full-brother, and Matthew and Samantha, the youngest of Ottie's children. Matthew is 18 and Samantha 20 years younger than me. Ottie and his wife Irene, who is six years younger than me, have no children. Ottie met Irene while being a driver at an Amish community. They fell in love and married. Her running away from the Amish, and the pursuit of her community, can be read in Ruth Irene Garrett's book *Crossing Over*. What an interesting family I have!

Ottie is a character, and can be overwhelming at times. He basically told me that he immediately wanted to get in the car and come and meet my family, and me, in person. I almost had a heart attack. I am a person who needs to think about things. I am the one who cannot show her emotion immediately after opening a present. That is why I always avoided bridal or baby showers. I hate being in the spotlight and needing to show all that happiness while everyone is watching. I would rather have people visit me individually and I can talk to them one by one and enjoy a nice peaceful time together. Anyway, Ottie's overwhelming way of wanting to jump into the car and come to meet us completely made me go into the defensive mode. With Edda it was such a nice slow time during which we wrote letters and met very sparsely, so we could get to know each other without hurry and faked emotions. I guess Ottie did realize my apprehension and he asked me if he could call me often from now on, maybe every week or so, to get to know me better. When I was ready, he would come. He had already planned to come with his wife, and maybe even Monte, my brother who is only six years younger than me. He seemed very fond of Monte, and I was excited to maybe meet him some day. With this, our first conversation ended, we had talked for over one hour.

CHAPTER 14

An Adventurous December

I felt exhausted after that one-hour telephone call, and asked Ross if he wanted a café latte. What a question. Asking Ross if he wants coffee is like asking a child if he wants candy. During the hot, long summers in Tucson though we learned to make iced latte with caramel syrup added as flavor. But this was a time where a nice hot latte, even at 110 degrees Fahrenheit, was a necessity. We sat in our nice, newly painted dining room and I told Ross all about my conversation with Ottie. The kids were playing in their room with play-dough on a little black and white table and the four animal-shaped chairs.

They loved the chairs and Sean chose the cat-like chair as his and Carmen the giraffe. Sean was now a little over two years old and had started to talk. Unfortunately, he spoke English more than German, but I was hoping he would learn the other language later, especially since I knew he understood me just perfectly. His hair was almost white-blond and very straight and Carmen's hair had started losing its wavy curls. It also changed its color slightly from the same white-blond Sean had now, to a more yellowish-blond with strands of various shades of blond. Ross's hair was still long, thick and brown and I had told him that cutting off his hair would be a reason for a divorce.

It was nice having a peaceful time of coffee and talking with Ross about Ottie. I could focus my thoughts and begin to comprehend all the things I had learned just then. I did not only have two mothers, now I had two fathers, too. It was kind of overwhelming, but I also felt an enormous relief. I was so lucky; I had heard other stories about adoptees that found their birth parents and were not welcomed at all. I seemed to be not only welcomed, but also loved by so many people. I had not expected Ottie to be so open, and so excited to meet me. Irene seemed to be a wonderful person as well. She did not mind at all that Ottie has a daughter who is six years older than her. On the contrary, she was very excited to meet me, hopefully soon.

My life seemed to have taken another turn. Although it seemed to be a good change, I felt lost and was not sure how to deal with all those new events. I also felt some sort of guilt. My mother had always been there for me, she had not minded when I found Edda, met her, wrote to her, and even visited my birth mother. Then I had to think about my father. He was deceased and now, I had a new father and it seemed not to be fair. I felt guilty, since my father could not "defend" himself, could not tell me it was okay to meet my biological father. I could not ask him if it was all right if I started a relationship with a person who, technically, was also my father. It did not seem fair.

Another burden, which weighed heavily on my heart, was that I had not told Edda yet that I found Ottie and had already contacted him. I was not sure how she would react, and I felt it was wrong that I had not told her. I really needed to change this and include her in these new events. Edda was so proud of me. She wrote in one recent letter that nothing better could have happened to her than to have given me life. Carmen sometimes draws a picture for Oma Edda and we would send it to her in a letter. This would make Edda so happy, and she would answer Carmen in a separate letter from mine and decorate the letter with beautiful little pictures she had drawn herself. Edda told us that her brother had been a very good artist. Edda was a loving grandmother and on many occasions told me how much she would love to watch the kids for me and live with us, but it was so far and so expensive. Edda even remembered our wedding day in July, which Ross and I usually forgot. If not for Ross's mom, who undoubtedly would call that day every year, we would completely forget our wedding anniversary. The four years had passed so quickly. Time seems to pass quickly once you have children, and nothing seems more important, and this is why you easily forget things like anniversaries.

In one of her letters, Edda told me when she realized for the first time that she was pregnant. Her mother had surgery, and Edda went with her to the town where the hospital was and stayed at a hotel. Edda took a week off to be close to her mother. She told me that she still has the nightgown she wore those thirty-something years ago in that hotel. She told me that, later on, when I was adopted, she would look at pictures of families and little children in magazines and would imagine it was me. Reading about her feelings, her loneliness, and her pain, always felt like somebody grabbed my heart and squeezed it tight. I wish I could give her that baby back, I wished I could be more of a daughter, but I was the daughter of someone else and that was where I belonged.

I was so busy thinking of my father and Edda that it struck me completely by surprise when I talked to my mother on the phone the following week. Suddenly my mother told me that now that I knew Ottie, she really did not want me to have any further contact with him! I was completely stunned. I had not expected this at all. My mother, who had been so cool and so relaxed with Edda, had a problem with Ottie. I could not really understand why, and asked. In my mother's mind, Ottie had the advantage of location, generally speaking, even though he was living in Kentucky. Though it was a good forty-hour drive from Tucson, compared to Germany, he was living close to us. She was afraid that he would take me away from her. I was stunned, and tried to understand her reasoning. The whole thing with Ottie had been so quick, and so out of her control. I did not have to look for him very long, and with his adventurous character and his open minded family, especially Irene, he had no problems meeting me and just taking me as his daughter. After all, he had many children who had all grown up with different mothers. For him, I was just a nice addition to the clan, and there was no secrecy and no delay through traveling over continents.

With Edda it had been a slow process, and because I was living abroad there was no danger of Edda coming between me and my mother, well, except maybe the wedding incident. And over the years, my mother had learned to accept our relationship and even form some sort of a friendship with Edda. Ottie, on the other hand, was not under her control. He could, and he most likely would, just come and visit and not care about what people said, and there was no secret about me between him and anybody else.

I told my mother calmly that nobody, never-ever, could come in between our relationship, and that she was always my mother, and my favorite one, too. I told her that now I could not turn back, that after writing him, I could not just simply disappear. It was my responsibility, and she had approved my letter to him. It was difficult, she accepted my argument, but in my heart I knew that she was suffering and that did not seem right. When I told her about my dilemma with my father and Ottie, and openly talked with her about my feelings, she seemed to calm down a little, but she was still somewhat apprehensive.

My companion in this situation, in addition to Ross of course, was Mandingo. I suddenly realized that my African brother by heart, Mandingo, also had several mothers he had grown up with. His father, though Catholic, had three wives at the same time. Mandingo's birth mother was the first and main wife, and Mandingo, as his oldest child and firstborn son, would become the patriarch of the family. Mandingo has fifteen siblings from those three wives, and is responsible for all of them, even though eight of them have different mothers. Mandingo told me that he calls all of his father's wives "mother," but that his late mother was the only real mother for him. Mandingo and I talked almost every day on the phone during this initial time of meeting Ottie, and his encouragement and knowledge of my strange family situations and how to handle them meant a lot to me. I had no idea how to handle all those parents and siblings. Although, I guess in modern times more and more family situations do include half-siblings, stepparents, and stepsiblings, my situation was a little different, since all those people were indeed related to me.

I was also concerned about my future relationship to my new siblings. Although Mandingo is not genetically related to me, we have a deep connection, as I have already explained. For over ten years now, we address each other as brother and sister, and frankly I did not want to call anybody else that. The term brother, to me, seemed to be reserved for my brother Christopher, of course, and to Mandingo, two people to which I felt deeply connected. I also learned with my sisters that calling somebody sibling does not make them become your soul mate. A relationship, any relationship, had to be established and fostered, and simply to name it a familiar name did not mean anything.

Finally, a few weeks after the initial call to Ottie, I could not delay a meeting anymore and we decided that Ottie, Irene, and Monte should visit us on December 26, the day after Christmas. Initially, they wanted to come for Christmas directly, but I was extremely hesitant to comply. After all, I did not even know them, and Christmas is a very special time for me. It is a magical time, particularly for children, and I did not want it to be interrupted by this visit. I felt that the day after Christmas was a more appropriate time. Their trip would include a 40-hour drive, and they would combine this long trip with a visit to Las Vegas. So it was settled. The Garrett clan would come for two days, and then continue their trip to Vegas.

Ottie seemed to love to eat, and he wanted to know if I could cook some traditional German food. I have to admit, I am not the best cook, but I do make a decent "goulash" and I am, with all due respect, an excellent baker. So a few days before they arrived, I started cleaning the house like crazy; after all, you cannot give a bad first impression to your own birth father. Saying that I was nervous was an absolute understatement. Baking and cooking kind of has the effect of distraction, so I baked two cakes and cooked like crazy. Ottie and Irene booked a hotel room in the hotel across the street and Monte was to stay in our guesthouse. Ottie needed a room with special amenities, but Monte should stay with us, so he could get to know us better. I think without Ottie's disability he would have stayed in our house as well, but to be honest I was kind of relieved that he was not staying here for this first meeting, since that way I could have some time to breathe.

The early afternoon of December 26, 2004 was a sunny and warm winter day in Tucson, Arizona. Suddenly, the phone rang. Ottie, Irene, and Monte had arrived at the hotel across the street and would be coming over to our house in a few minutes. My heart was racing. This was it. I would get to know the last puzzle piece in the origin of my existence. Suddenly, we could hear the gravel in the driveway making the sound of tires driving over them, and the kids darted to the window. There is a big window in our living room, right behind the couch, which leads to the half-circle gravel driveway enclosing a part of our front yard I called the cactus island. It had two palo verde trees, an organ pipe cactus, an ocotillo, two barrel cacti, and lots of other desert plants. During the spring, the organ pipe cactus would bloom early in the morning with the biggest yellowish-white flowers you can imagine. The flowers would only open up early in the morning and had three rows of about four inches long and one-inch wide petals with a center of long-stemmed seeds.

I went to the door and opened it. My heart seemed to be beating in my neck. I saw Ottie looking out his van window and taking a picture of the kids curiously peeking out from behind the curtain. I went to the big white van in front of our house. Almost shyly, I said hello. Irene came around the van and gave me a hug. She was a nice-looking woman, thirty-one years old, just six years younger than me. She radiated a natural kindness with a winning smile, and I just had to like her instantaneously. Monte also got out of the car, and after a quick hello, he started unloading the wheelchair for Ottie. They brought the wheelchair into the house and then Irene helped

Ottie out of the van. With the help of his cane, he came up the three red steps into the house. Then he sat safely in his wheelchair Monte had placed in the living room.

I have to admit, I have never in my life seen a man that size before, but Ottie's personality makes you forget his size immediately. First he told me,

"Now let me look at you and hug you. My sister Faye told me not to forget to give you at least one great hug."

And so we hugged. Sean was a little scared of all those people at first, but that changed very quickly when Ottie introduced the kids to the "invisible ball in the bag." I have to tell you, a small paper bag and some rustling noise, combined with a convincible notion that there is indeed a ball in it you can throw in the air and would land right back in the paper bag with a noise, is all it takes to entertain kids for hours.

According to German tradition, we had coffee and cake first. It was afternoon and the dinner was happily cooking by itself in the crock-pot. Ottie is such a character that all possible awkward moments were immediately gone. He brought tons of pictures and Monte even copied me a family tree dating back to the sixteen hundreds! My family was Irish and Welsh. And ... I could not believe it when I heard it the first time ... Cherokee! Me, a German blond woman, was not only American, I was part Native American! It was a dream come true. Ottie had even brought me a picture of my great-great-great-grandmother, which made me 1/32 Cherokee; not bad for a German, whose dream had been during all her childhood, yeah and adulthood, to be part Native American. I have to go and buy some books and learn about my heritage!

Irene had lots of fun with the kids. She loves children, but sadly, even after having so many children before, now Ottie seemed to not be able to have any more. How strange fate is; finally he had found the woman of his life, and now they could not have any children. I liked Irene immediately, and her happy and soulful character was part of why this whole meeting seems easy and relaxed.

Monte is a fun person also. He seemed like a gentle giant to me. He is so much taller and bigger than me, and has long red hair like a Viking. He has tattoos all over his arms and drives a big Harley Davidson. In contrast, he loves to cook and when he left the little guesthouse after the two days he had been living there, it was clean and the bed made! Although I had been worried, I liked Monte right away. It was a different kind of relationship though than with my sisters. We did not pretend to be brother and sister, we did not try to compare possible similarities in character or physical characteristics, we just hung out. Monte is used to having siblings from different mothers, and for him, despite the fact that it was cool to have a real German sister, it was not so different than with his other siblings. Monte had not been at all surprised when he heard that he had an older sister. Since I was the only sibling his age, he was curious to meet me, and in a way, I was exotic to him. I was glad he came, and was hoping we could become friends. There was no pressure. I was just surprised to hear that Monte did not really interact with his younger siblings, Matthew and Samantha, although they did not live so far from him in Indiana. They were so young, he said, and did not have anything in common with him. But they are your siblings I interjected. Maybe he should have some more contact, he thought.

I could not help but like Ottie. He was such a fun person and really got around considering his disabilities. He basically cannot be in one place for too long. Does that sound familiar? He used to be an architect and a photographer, and he could not believe the pictures I used to take on my trips to Argentina and Europe. I am quite proud of them I have to admit. Ottie and Irene brought some presents for us. Carmen got her first Barbie doll, a singing Cinderella, which she admired a lot, although she did not know who Cinderella was. But the singing made the day. Sean got a train to go around the Christmas tree; being a little train enthusiast, exactly what a little two-year-old dreams of. Ross and I received an absolutely gorgeous white quilt with blue designs. It was so beautiful and handcrafted by an Amish woman, that I could never really use it to cover our bed, because the dog and cat hair would ruin it.

That first day with the Garretts went by way too fast. We had dinner that day and shortly after Ottie and Irene went to the hotel to get some sleep, and Monte did not stay up long either. He is a pipe-fitter, and used to having to get up very early in the morning, so he got in the habit of going to bed early too.

The following morning we had breakfast, but I am sad to say that I think those heavenly Swedish pancakes Ross makes did not fit their hearty appetite so much. I think, being from the South, they prefer their eggs with ham for the beginning of the day. Our cafe latte also did not get the deserved applause; Ottie loves coffee, but just simple strong coffee. Well, I learned for the next time. After breakfast, we went out to the Tucson Mountain Park to show them some real cacti. Ottie stayed in the car and I asked Monte why Ottie would not come out to see better. Monte told me that Ottie is so conscious of his size that he just stays in his big van and enjoys the scenery through the open window. Monte assured me that Ottie did not mind being alone in the van, while we walked around the park's museum a little, that Ottie had been doing this for a very long time. I felt sad for Ottie, while we were having fun and watching the movie about the Sonoran Desert, Ottie was alone in his van.

The next stop of our one-day tour of the Sonoran Desert was, of course, San Xavier, "The white dove of the desert," the beautiful Tohono O'Odham Nation Church. The Mission, San Xavier del Bac, was first built by Father Eusebio Kino in 1700. The present church was built from 1783-1797. San Xavier is acclaimed to be the finest example of mission architecture in the United States. It is located in the Santa Cruz Valley, nine miles south of Tucson. Ross, the kids, Irene, Monte, and I went inside the Mission Church and the little museum which is associated with the church.

After that we were ready for some real Mexican food! Tucson has some of the best Mexican food outside Mexico; Ross and I are sure about this! Although the Garretts could not eat as spicy as we were used to, they loved the food and the ambience. After dinner, we went back home and Ottie and Irene retired to their hotel room. Early the next morning they left as fast as they had come. Those had been two very exciting days, and it would take me weeks to get this all sorted out and digested. I learned about so many new people, and even talked with my new Aunt Faye, Ottie's sister, on the phone. Regrettably, Ottie told me that for a year his relationship to his father had deteriorated. The two had been very close for most of their lives, but something had happened, which had spoiled their relationship. I could not believe it, there I come from across the ocean to make peace and mend the strings that were cut over thirty years prior and are willing to start anew and forget the past, and there they are, living just a block apart and not talking to each other. That had to change.

Ottie begged us to come to Kentucky as soon as possible, but Ross was about to graduate and was in his final stages of writing his dissertation. To make any kind of plans involving traveling seemed too far removed for Ross at this point. I was kind of relieved for this delay as well, since it gave me some more time to digest our first visit and to develop a closer relationship with Ottie via the phone. But I was excited to go to Kentucky in the near future to meet the rest of the clan.

After Ottie, Irene, and Monte left, I had to think about Edda, and that she had no idea what happened in the meantime and so far away from Germany. I did not want to hurt her feelings, but this was part of me too. I just had to do this. I talked to my mother about the situation. My mother told me that she talked to Edda about Ottie and Edda had told my mother that in her mind Ottie was dead. My mother did not think Edda wanted her old wounds reopened by knowing I had contact with him. I thought about that, but I felt so uneasy that, one day in January 2005, I called Edda to tell her about Ottie. My dear sister Amelie told me that her father was swimming that day, so I could talk to our mother without him hearing our conversation. It took all my courage to call. Well, what can I say, my courage left me when I talked to her and I hung up after talking about this and that and not about Ottie! Shame on me!

On my thirty-seventh birthday, eight years after I met Edda, her husband wrote me a special birthday card. He told me that he was so happy I had come into their lives and he was impressed by my caring and nice personality. All in all, he was happy that I existed. It was so nice and kind of him to write this to me. Once again, I questioned if he was really the way his family had portrayed him to me or if they actually misunderstood him.

A few weeks after my call to Edda, I finally sat down and composed a letter. It took me quite some time to write it, and in it I told her all about my feeling of wanting to know where I came from. I wrote that I did not intend to hurt her, or change any of my feelings towards her. I told her all about Ottie's previous marriages and children and concluded that if she had married him thirty-eight years ago, it might have been likely that they would have been divorced, and she would be living in a foreign country as a single mother. I told her that I thought that she was very well off with Karl, who, I was sure loved her very much, and that they had a good life with healthy, loving children and that she should be so grateful for this.

It took almost two months until Edda had the chance to read the letter while visiting Sophie, where I sent the letter. Sophie, as you might know, knew about me writing and meeting Ottie, since I stayed in close contact with my sisters and told them about finally sending the letter they helped compose to him. Edda answered that she knew that I wanted to meet my father and get to know him too. She told me that this was why she kept his picture and address in the first place and had eventually given it to me. She was surprised to hear that it was the chaplain who did not agree to the wedding, and even considered that in that case she had done Ottie wrong by hating him so much. My sisters, though, had a totally different opinion. They thought that Ottie was a chicken for not going against his chaplain. They thought Ottie should have fought more against the army and somehow got a message to Edda. I asked Ottie about it, and his answer was that if you went against the army you could be imprisoned or released without honors, which had very bad consequences. He also did not know her home address. The whole affair was the result of some very tragic and unforeseen events, I concluded.

I started feeling resentment for that chaplain, however. How many lives had this person destroyed being stationed in Germany and sending young pregnant women to their doom? I would still like to meet him and give him a piece of my mind, but I might never be able to do so. Edda just did not understand why Ottie had not sent a message to her through his friend, like he had done previously. She believed that her father, who was a friend of the commander in that army base, could have made a difference. Poor Edda never did tell her parents that she was expecting, since she felt so ashamed. She cried so much when she went to the lawyer to sign the final papers of my adoption. I felt blameworthy to have awakened all those old emotions again, and her pain, which had partially ceased because I had come back. Edda's only hope throughout those twenty-nine years without me had been that my parents were kind and loving and that I had a good, safe home. She was so thankful for my parents, but she also told me that Ottie could never make things good again. Why had he never sent her a message? In those days she could still speak English and write it too. She was a babysitter for an American family, and her English was better at that time. She made me promise to never let Ottie know her address or new name, because he could never contact her. I understood her and I swore not to break my promise.

Edda went on dreaming about how nice everything could have been without all these events. She could be with me now, with her grandchildren instead of having to denying my existence. She cried while she wrote the letter, and had to stop writing because she was shaken from all the old memories.

What could I do to make her happy? I signed the letter "your daughter Julia" and Edda told me that she cried when she read this. Although I did not address her with "mother," I felt that I should show her I did think of her as something special in my life, my birth mother.

In April of 2005, Ross completed his dissertation and passed his dissertation defense. He was now an official Ph.D. We sent formal graduation cards to friends and family, including Ottie and Edda. Edda had some time to adjust to all the new events and information, and in her letter thanked us for this nice graduation card, she also told me that she was feeling much better now. I was so relieved.

In May, the graduation ceremony was held. Without telling Ross, I invited his mother, brother, Vargus, Ricki and Julie from Illinois, and organized a surprise party at our house. The party was a great success. Ross could not believe how many people had shown up, and that his childhood friend, Ricki, and his wife, Julie, had also flown into town just for him. And despite the fact that Julie absolutely despises flying! It was a great party out in the yard with many friends we had not seen in a long time. Little did we know that this was also the last time we would see all those people together, for some of them, it was the last time we saw them at all.

CHAPTER 15

Back to the Roots

Ottie finally got his wish. His graduation gift to Ross was four airplane tickets to Kentucky! Oh, that is so typical of him! Now we could no longer procrastinate. My parents had always called me stubborn. Well, I now know where I got that from. And this is how, in the middle of June 2005, the four of us took the airplane from Tucson to Nashville, Tennessee.

I was excited and nervous at the same time. Although I had dreamed about this moment for a long time, I had been avoiding this trip for a few months now, until I could evade it no more. This situation was almost more than I could handle. I can be very emotional, and there were so many people to meet. Meeting Edda and her family was so much slower. I had time to adjust first to her alone, then to her husband, two years later, and then to my sisters, one after the other. Ottie's family, on the other hand, was big and they all wanted to meet me. There was not only Ottie and Irene and Monte. There was my sister Samantha, my brother Matthew, my Aunt Faye, her two children, my Uncle Bennie and his family, my grandfather and his wife, and as far as I understood, lots of first and second cousins. A big party was planned to introduce us to Ottie's extended family and friends. I was a little nervous about how those people, whose genes I carry, would react to me, and how they would accept me. In addition, I learned by meeting my birth mother and her family, that things are not always as easy and simple as they originally seem. It is not an effortless task to combine two, well three, families with two mothers and two fathers and about ten siblings without neglecting, or hurting, or misjudging some of the involved family members.

Finally, we arrived at the airport in Nashville. Irene was already waiting for us at the baggage claim area. The kids recognized her immediately, and felt totally comfortable with her. They ran to her and hugged her as if they had known her all their lives. We got our luggage and went outside. Ottie was waiting in his big van just outside the doors. I was happy to see him, although I still did not really know how to act around him. It was a strange situation. This was my birth father, and unlike the situation with Edda, he told everybody who wanted or did not want to hear, that I was his daughter from Germany. The trip from Nashville to Glasgow, Kentucky takes about 1.5 hours, and Ottie used the time to acquaint me with the people I was about to meet. He made me sit in the front seat next to him, so we could talk better to each other, while the kids absolutely enjoyed Irene's company in the back of the spacious vehicle. Ross just sat there and listened. He was very patient the whole trip, but I think he had fun meeting all those people. He mentioned to me on the plane how interesting it was that my birth family, in a way, was not that much different than his family. Both lived in small communities and their lives were very similar.

The landscape was so amazing to me, so green and lush, and so different from Arizona. I had been in Tennessee once before during a three-month trip through the U.S. in 1990 with my friends, but once you have lived in the desert for eight years, those dense green colors are amazingly beautiful. The small rolling hills also gave such a rich, almost peaceful appearance. It felt like I could take a deep breath and just hold the fresh air in my lungs. I had never really adjusted to the lack of green grass, and I missed that the most living in Tucson.

Ottie told me about his seventy-seven year old father, Ottie Sr. Although father and son did not talk to each other at this point, my grandfather was eager to meet me and was very excited to have another granddaughter and two new great-grandchildren. Faye, Ottie's younger sister, he informed me, liked to talk, but had a good heart. His youngest daughter, Samantha, was eighteen years old and had been the princess of the family. She was not only his youngest; she also had been his only daughter until recently. She came to stay with Ottie and Irene from her mother's house in Indiana, just to meet me and my family. Ottie told me that Sam was excited to meet me, but saw me as a kind of a competition. Thinking about me as competition though, made me laugh. Samantha was, after all, twenty years younger than me and could, technically, be my daughter.

Matthew, Ottie's nineteen-year-old son, had just recently moved to Kentucky from Indiana. He was trying to finish his high school degree since he and his sister Samantha had never really gone to school. He had lived with Ottie and Irene before, after Ottie and his mother divorced, but had moved back to his mother's in the interim. Monte, who I already knew, came from his home in Indiana to see Ross, the kids, and me again.

When we finally arrived at the white, three bedroom, ranch-style house, all my half-siblings were waiting for us. Samantha seemed shy and left the room several times while we were sitting in the nicely decorated living room. She somehow seemed uncomfortable with this new situation. I could not really blame her. She was slightly taller and than me, had black, died, shoulder-length hair and very white skin. Her eyes were dark and narrow, but since she avoided direct eye contact, it was hard to tell. She gave me some really nice earrings in the shape of dream catchers, which I really loved. She bought them from a Native American friend. I had bought her a cute little flax purse. I did not know her, and I thought since I love purses so much, this is what I should give her. We later found out that Sam is dyslexic, like me, but loves to write poetry. She gave me something to read and, although I liked it, Ottie was right, it was pretty dark poetry. I am not very good at metaphors and poetry as a result, but I think Sam is talented, and just needs some guidance. That was the general impression I had about her, a young girl in desperate need of guidance for her life. I did not know how growing up with her divorced parents and her mother moving a lot would be, but I could tell that she was lacking stability in her life.

Monte seemed really happy to see us again, and I liked him even better than before. I had bought him a Tohono O'Odham necklace with the "path of life" depicted on it, and he really seemed to love it. After all, he was with us at the reservation in December. For Matthew, I bought a University of Arizona baseball hat. Matthew seemed to be really easy-going. He likes to collect things, especially old money and Civil War items. He is a very sweet and caring person. When he realized the kids liked to watch some kids' shows on TV he bought them *Dora* tapes. I also was impressed about the nice things he said about Sam, how nice she was and how pretty. Sam, herself, seemed to think that she was the "black sheep," an outsider in the family, which I think she, in part, had created herself.

When Matthew and I had the chance to drive in his car together alone, he told me:

"I wish I could have seen you grow up." It took me by surprise and I started laughing and said:

"Matthew, that is very nice of you. But guess what, even if we would have grown up in the same household, you would have never seen me grow up, since I am eighteen years older than you." But his sweetness and the sincerity of his wish really touched my heart.

We arrived on a Friday in Glasgow, Kentucky and for Sunday, a big barbeque was planned. Lots of family members and some good friends were invited. My Aunt Faye came early, and immediately fell in love with the children, who, in turn, absolutely adored her. It was funny, not only was her name Faye, like Kay, Ross's mother's name, but she also had bleached-blond hair, loved pink, and angels. I was fascinated by those similarities. Her children, my cousins, are Alex and Angel, two very nice people in their early 30s. Alex is a very funny guy and I liked him instantly. He has an eleven-year-old son Anthony, which he raised without a mother, being just a perfect father. I have the utmost respect for that. Alex's sister, Angel, a very blond Kentucky girl, with an accent I could barely understand, had an eight-year-old son named Skyler.

I had seen all of those people in pictures before, but to meet them in person was great. Even Ottie's brother, Ben, and his wife, Sharon, came to the barbeque. Ben was a pleasant guy, and said he was relieved that, finally, someone in this family spoke "real" English. Not to offend anyone, and as a German Native speaker, I do not know what real English is supposed to be, I just know that even a few years ago, I would have not understood even a single word anybody was saying in Kentucky.

After the barbeque, Ottie, Irene, Faye, Alex, Angel, Monte, Sam, and all of us sat on the deck outside talking and having fun. It was a great evening, warm, but not too hot, the air was a little moist, but did not come even close to the humidity one could have expected during the summer in Kentucky. Ross had so much fun, especially with Alex, that I started to wonder if he was the one related to them or me. I guess he was right, this family was almost like the family he had grown up with. And I had grown up in a completely different cultural background. I really enjoyed all their company. It was so relaxing, and Ross and Alex had competitions in who could tell the funniest stories. It was strange to me to realize that, even though I had grown up in Germany, I had chosen a husband who grew up in a family not much different from my own biological family. On the other hand, we both are kind of the oddballs in the family: Ross, a farm boy with a Ph.D., and me, a German with a Masters degree, in the hinterland of Kentucky. Strangely enough, I felt right at home. Everything was so easy here. There were no secrets, everybody knew who I was, and even further, Ottie introduced me proudly as his daughter to everybody who wanted or did not want to know. Everybody was so proud of me as Ottie's daughter, the Ph.D. candidate with the Ph.D. husband and the cutest grandchildren. How different this experience was from meeting Edda and her family. With Ottie and Irene, we could talk about the old times, about what happened in Germany. Ottie told me how he loved the time in Germany, it was the best days of his life! Irene did not mind at all, and was really cool about it. I admired her stamina, after all, she had not even been born yet when that happened. Ottie, I could tell, was really in love with Irene, which he should be, and therefore, there was nothing for Irene about which to be jealous.

I had fun with Irene's German, which most people, for some reason, call Pennsylvanian Dutch. She used some words that I knew from the dialect my father's relatives spoke in a rural area of Germany called Hunsrück. For example, she called potatoes, which are called "Kartoffeln" in German "Krumbeere," which is exactly the word my father's relatives use. I wanted to show her how it looks in that particular region in Germany, but the only picture of this area I found in the picture book I gave them was from Koblenz, a bigger city at the border of this region. Irene's eyes lit up; Koblenz was a common last name in her community. "Well, there we go," I could say using Ross's famous words.

The next day Monte, Sam, Matthew, Ross, the kids, and I visited Great-Grandpa Ottie and his wife Pat. He and my grandmother divorced when Ottie was just a child, and Pat was his second wife. They were both really nice, and I have to say I really took to my grandfather. He is a great person and has done so much in his life, considering he only had a third grade education and left home when he was just fifteen! He had done many things, like building race cars, bootlegging, managing a gas station, a farm, and finally an excavating business. Now he was finally thinking of retiring and spending the rest of his life with his wife. He told us that life passes so fast and you work and work and work and suddenly, forty years have gone and you forgot to live. He regretted that, and wanted us to not make the same mistake. He is a wise person, and had lots of cool stories to tell about his life and life in general.

We took some beautiful photographs with him, and I am proud to say that I somewhat look like him. He repeated how proud he was of me, and our kids, and how much he hoped that we would come back, and he would love to come and visit us. Too bad that he and my birth father were not speaking to one another. I felt bad for both of them.

Somehow, dealing with my grandfather was much easier than with my birth father. Maybe it was because there was no feeling of guilt, no competition. I never had a grandfather, since my mother's father died around the time I was born, and my father was raised by a single mother. I could totally enjoy having a grandfather now, and such a nice one. Ottie Sr. captured my heart completely when he told me what a good job my mother had done raising me, that I was so kind and forgiving to come all the way from Germany to become part of their family. I was so impressed that he was the only one thus far who had considered that I had another family in another country, and that it was not taken for granted that I had come back without resentment and embraced my new-old family.

Ottie Sr., my grandfather, loved trucks, and so did Sean. Little Sean was absolutely ecstatic to see great-grandpa's big red pickup truck, which he kept safe from weather and reckless drivers in his downstairs garage. He did not trust his grandchildren to drive this car everybody admired, and hid his truck out of fear they will wreck it. Great-grandpa told me that his grandsons did not have a good reputation for driving cars, and I heard some very interesting driving and crashing stories.

The following Sunday was Father's Day. That was kind of strange to be in the house of my birth father and to celebrate Father's Day. When I went to bed the night before, I had to think about my father and how unfair it was that he had never seen my wedding, and never met our beautiful children. He would have been so proud and happy. It was painful to think that we were here with Ottie to celebrate Father's Day, while my father was deceased.

We took beautiful pictures of all of us: Ottie with Irene and all his children, and Ottie with us. Matthew, Monte, and I went to the local Walmart to enlarge the two best pictures and have them framed. They looked absolutely gorgeous. Then we presented them to Ottie as a Father's Day gift. Ottie was very emotional about this gift, and he hung the pictures in his living room, so everybody who came to visit would see them immediately.

The trip was over very fast and I was feeling like I was in a dream, or a strange movie. I tried to hide my feelings a little while I was in Kentucky, because, honestly, I did not really know what to think. I was happy and excited and relieved, but at the same time I felt almost guilty for Edda. Why is my relationship to her family so complicated, so secretive, and with Ottie it is so easy? I called my mother when we got home to Tucson and talked with her about it. She assured me that there was no need to feel guilty. Unfortunately, I did not have much time to think about it and to come to a conclusion, because events suddenly occurred with an enormous speed and turned our lives completely around.

We came back on a Wednesday afternoon, and on that Friday at work, Ross's boss told him that he was running short of funding and that he had to lay him off. He could give Ross three months to find a new job before he had to leave. I remember it like yesterday. Ross came home from work, looking rather normal. While I was making dinner he nonchalantly mentioned that he had two pieces of news: he would be laid off in three months and that maybe this was finally the time to leave Tucson. Ross and I had been planning on leaving for quite a while. We thought about Germany and Canada, but both places seemed not to work, so Ross had the idea to use his grandmother's empty house in Belvidere and live there until he found a job in the Midwest, preferably in Madison, Wisconsin. We both loved Madison; Ross for quite some time, and I since I first went there to my cousin's wedding in 1999. I was fine with the idea of leaving Tucson, since we could never pay the mortgage of our beautiful house with the unemployment money, or even a post-doc salary. We barely got along as it was.

Being who we are, Ross and I started planning the details

of selling our house and moving. His mother was delighted to have us close to her, and so we started thinking of how to best sell the house. The housing market was good at that time, but we did not know then how good it actually was, and how close to a crash. We told our friends we were leaving and started selling baby items we did not want to take along. And guess what, one of our friends, who we called to ask if he needed a crib, did not buy the crib, but instead bought the house! We had our house sold not even a week after Ross had gotten the notice of being laid off. Ross and I were excited, and we decided that he should work the full three months to save as much money as we could. The kids and I would be leaving a few weeks before Ross to go to Illinois, since school started before Ross's three months were up, and Carmen had to start kindergarten. So the next few weeks we packed and arranged the house, and registered Carmen for kindergarten in Belvidere, Illinois. After I left, Ross was supposed to drive the moving truck, pulling our car, with the help of his brother and his friend, Ricardo the forty-some hours from Arizona to Illinois.

CHAPTER 16

Life in the Little House

Time seemed to fly by after the decision was made to leave Tucson. The two months until the kids, Puck, and I took the airplane to Chicago were filled with packing, organizing, and saying goodbyes.

Sean's third birthday served as the official goodbye party. I had not realized how many good friends we had in Tucson, until they all showed up to tell how much they would miss us. It would be sad to leave them behind. After all, Tucson was the place where it had all begun, where Ross and I met, where we bought our first home, where I had given birth to our children. A part of our life was now over and a new chapter would begin.

Puck was in a cat carrier underneath my seat and he meowed basically the whole four-hour plane flight. Kay picked us up in Chicago with her big, old, yellow and red van. The van is so old and so rusted that every time we came to visit her, we thought that this time for sure the van must be completely broken, but somehow Ross's brother Grant managed to make that old vehicle street-worthy.

Kay drove right to her late mother's little house, which she calls the "doll house." It is about 800 square feet and is filled with furniture. Kay had lovingly prepared the house, but unfortunately, there was not so much room for our things, since most of the cabinets were still filled. The living room was nice and surprisingly spacious and the kitchen was small, but had a little table in it. There was an addition, which served as the dining room, where I set up my workplace in the attempt to finally finish my dissertation. Ross and I had planned that while he was looking for a job and staying home, he could be helping with Sean and the housework, so that I could finally have time to work on my dissertation.

The kids loved to have Grandma close by, and did not mind the lack of space. A part of me felt lonely and sad, being here in a town where I barely found my way around, without Ross, in a little house, which was not mine, and a child who had to start school in three days, a school about which I knew nothing. In Tucson, we had carefully looked at several schools, including a Montessori and a Magnet school, and Carmen was accepted to all of them. Kay left me one of her cars. I was grateful that Kay had given us the house to live in for free, just needing to pay the utilities, but everything felt so unreal and unfamiliar.

Kay had signed Carmen up for the Meehan Elementary School in Belvidere, a school within walking distance from our new little house. After we arrived on Sunday, Carmen, Sean, and I visited the school on Monday morning. School was about to begin on that Wednesday. It seemed to have a friendly environment and the principal greeted us warmly and we even got to meet Carmen's future teacher. She was a very pleasant person, and I was glad that Carmen would be in good hands. I did not know anything about the schools in Belvidere, but I soon realized that this particular school, in this school district, was one of the best in Illinois. Kay came the morning of the first day of school, and the four of us walked to the school together. It was hot, and Carmen wore a new cute little pink dress, which she had chosen. It was a good walk, and I was glad that we did not have to drive or for Carmen to take the bus, although that was Carmen's big dream. She told me several times that, if we would move again, to please move to some place where she could take a school bus, just like the other children.

On October 2, a Saturday and two weeks after we had arrived in Belvidere, Ross, Grant and Ricardo, with help of some of our friends in Tucson, packed the moving truck and headed toward the Midwest. It would take them until Tuesday morning to arrive at the farm, without any nights of sleep. Xenon was with them. I had considered taking Xenon in the plane with me, but she was older now, over ten years old, and after consulting a veterinarian we decided that it would be too stressful for her to fly. Xenon would be terrified, and possibly have heart failure if we would subject her to such a strenuous trip. Riding along with the moving truck seemed a much better idea.

When Ross, Grant, and Ricardo finally arrived at the farm, they pretty much looked like zombies. Their eyes looked big and tired after no real sleep for three days, and they all started to grow shaggy beards. Ross's birthday was the following day, but he pretty much just relaxed and slept on that day. It was his fortieth birthday, and for a special treat I made reservations for the two of us to go to Chicago and stay at a hotel the following weekend. The kids would be at the farm and spend the time with Grandma. It was a nice and relaxing weekend, which both of us surely deserved.

My mother and I talked about twice a week on the phone, which was a big comfort for me. One day in October, she told me that she talked to Edda at length that day. I liked the fact that my "two mothers" had become something like friends and I had the feeling that my birth mother sought out my mother's advice in issues concerning me, my birth father, and even Karl. This time Edda told my mother that Karl sold their beautiful little house in northern Germany and they would be moving to Bad Kreuznach, a town only twenty miles west of my mother's house. They would be renting an apartment there. Edda did not seem very happy about this development: it seemed her husband had decided this major event in their lives without her consent. They would even be selling their car, since in Bad Kreuznach a car is not really necessary, considering the convenient location of stores and the favorable bus and train services.

I was surprised to hear this news. First of all, I knew Edda really liked the place where they were living, and second of all, for the choice of town her husband had made. Bad Kreuznach, you have to realize, is the very town where I was born and where I had grown up the first nine years of my life. That was a strange coincidence, and I had to wonder if her husband knew about that. Edda's sister also lived there, and they had not talked in some years for reasons I did not know. I was hoping that if Edda really moved there she and her sister could start a new relationship. Edda told my mother how upset she was about moving and especially moving there, but that the only good thing was that now she could come visit my mother from time to time, since the two towns were only fifteen minutes apart by train.

From my point of view, I would love for Edda to move closer to my mother's house. I could visit them more easily, and did not have to travel a whole day. I could just come by for an afternoon for coffee and cake. I could visit more frequently and maybe just go shopping with Edda some day. It also occurred to me that maybe, since nobody really knew Edda and her husband there, she could finally tell people that they had four daughters, instead of three. And she could finally tell people that she had grandchildren. That was such a nice thought and I decided to talk to my sisters about this idea. Ross, the cynic, thought Karl would most likely not allow this to happen.

A few days later I got a letter from Edda in which she told me about their plans of moving. And … that Christine had talked to Karl about the situation with me and that most likely she did not have to hide me anymore! I started to cry, that is how much this new development touched me. What a wonderful thought. I cared so much for her and I felt so bad that Ottie could have all the fun being a grandfather, while she could not even proudly show anyone the pictures of her grandchildren. I would be so happy for her and so relieved. After all, I still had friends in that town myself, and I would not pretend she was just my distant relative or friend. I was already getting excited about my next trip to Germany to start a real relationship with Edda, with an open acknowledgment. It would mean a new beginning of our connection. My heart was filled with joy, maybe things would work out after all, maybe somehow the pain could be taken from her and she could start a new life.

The following day I called Sophie and talked with her about the new development. Sophie told me that all three of my sisters talked to their father, telling him that they did not make any secret of having a fourth sister and asked their father why he could not accept me officially as part of their family. They proposed that when their parents moved it would be a good time to just tell people they had four daughters.

Sophie also seemed to be really relieved for her parents to move to Bad Kreuznach. It is a picturesque smaller city where everything is close together and, being independent of a car, it might give Edda the opportunity to do things on her own, like volunteering at the Elderly Home, and having coffee with my mother. This was not possible where they lived before because there were all small villages without public transportation and Edda, who does not drive, was always dependent on her husband to drive her around.

My two mothers started some sort of a friendly relationship in the meantime. Who would have thought it possible after the wedding disaster? I really hoped everything would work out now and I could already imagine myself going shopping with Edda and having coffee with her in a coffee shop without Karl. It is not that I did not like him, to the contrary, I believe Edda is very fortunate to have him, but we should really have some time alone, to really talk about our feelings, our dreams, our future and … Ottie.

One sunny, warm day in October 2005, Ottie and Irene finally came to visit us in the little house. Compared to the trip to Tucson, this was only a ten-hour drive, and with Ottie loving to drive so much, it seemed to be a much better deal than us living in Tucson. Monte was also supposed to come. He still lives in Indiana, about halfway between Ottie's and our home. I was still a little ambiguous about my relationship to Ottie. I knew that he did not have any bad intention when he had left Edda alone, and I also knew he really wanted to make up for the time he had lost with me not seeing me grow up. On the other hand, it was hard to forget how much pain he had cost

Edda. I truly liked Ottie, but it is still strange to think of him as my father. My father had died almost seven years ago, and nobody can ever replace him. It is my father who should have been the one seeing his grandchildren grow up, and I could not help but wonder what he would think about Ottie.

It was an unusually warm and pleasant day for October, a day like you picture an Indian summer. The sky was bright, and the trees had started changing the colors of their leaves in all imaginable shades of yellow, orange, and red. It was a wonderful sensation to hear the geese flying due south over the roofs of the houses. It seemed so long since I had heard their cries announcing the change in season. I had almost forgotten how beautiful and almost enchanted fall was. Tucson basically only had two seasons: summer and winter, whereas winter was almost like spring, since the temperatures never really went below 50 degrees Fahrenheit and the sun would almost always shine. In Illinois, we had visited the apple orchard already several times, and had picked black raspberries in the backyard of the little house. I had not realized how much I had missed the four seasons while living in Tucson. Now I almost overly enjoyed the changes in temperature, as well as flora and fauna.

I cleaned the house the day before they would arrive, and baked and prepared food. I wanted the little house to be as inviting and clean as possible. The day of their arrival, I was ready and the only thing left to do was to wait. I wanted them to come, right now. To ease my nerves, I left the house to buy some milk at the grocery store. When I came back Ross told me that they had finally arrived at the hotel where they would be staying, and were getting ready to come over. This house is way too small for visitors to stay, but Monte had decided to sleep on a mattress in the living room. Ottie and Irene would stay in a hotel nearby. I kind of liked that arrangement: that way we had a little space left for ourselves. I really wanted to get to know Monte better, and I was glad that he decided to stay with us. I hoped some day he would come visit us by himself, so we could get to know him without other people around. After all, we were close in age, and it would be nice to do things and talk about things people our age would do. I think Ottie would like that too; I think he wanted us to become friends, because Monte had lost Philip as a sibling his age, and Matthew and Samantha were so much younger than us. Ottie had specially rearranged his visit to accommodate Monte's work schedule.

After what seemed an eternity, they finally arrived at our house. It was early afternoon, just the right time to have coffee and cake. My German almond cake was very well received, and the atmosphere was nice and relaxed. An hour after the Garretts arrived, Vargus, Kay, and a friend came for dinner. I wanted them to get to know Ottie, to make the situation as normal as possible and start the integration process of those two families. Carmen was overwhelmed by so many people, and she hid for a long time in her room. Finally, she warmed up and spent time with her two grandmothers.

We talked about a lot of things during dinner, but one topic was my half-brother Matthew. He started college again and had to take English composition. One of his papers was supposed to be about a family member and their education. And Ottie said kind of disappointed:

"He did not chose me and he also passed Irene, the bestselling author, but instead he chose you."

According to Ottie, Matthew wrote all about me being an archaeologist with high academic degrees from Germany and America; his sister with a real German passport, who had lived and worked in Argentina, and who had a husband who recently completed a Ph.D. His story was so fantastic that his classmates did not believe him, until he showed them a picture of us! That was very amusing to me. I never considered myself as being so exotic to my siblings. We got a great kick out of this story. In Matthew's eyes, his new sister was some sort of an Indiana Jones! I have to say, even though nothing in the movie really reflects what archaeologists actually do, I felt proud and honored by this comparison. Years later, Vargus gave me my very own Indiana Jones hat as a gift!

The following morning, Carmen and Sean got up at 7 a.m. and, as usual wanted to watch *Thomas the Train* on the TV in the living room. Then they realized with astonishment that Monte's mattress was occupying most of the floor in the room. At first they were a little shy, sneaking around the mattress, but after about ten minutes, Ross and I suddenly heard a thump. The kids were jumping up and down on Monte's mattress, with him still sleeping on it. They were having a blast waking up the sleepy Uncle Monte. Later on, I tried to explain to Carmen that Monte is also my brother, kind of like Christopher. They call all of our friends aunt and uncle, so when I told Carmen that Monte was my brother, she answered that she did not know that. It is strange, on one hand I want Monte to be my brother, but on the other hand, I do not want to take away Christopher's privileges as my only brother. It is really complicated. Or is it just me who cannot adapt? Why do I always have to feel guilty? I guess I want to protect my family, keep them special, let them know that they are the most important people to me. But how do I do this?

During our conversations, Ottie suddenly expressed his wish to go with Irene to visit Germany. I think my heart stopped for a beat or two when I heard him say this. His dream was for Irene to get to know the country of the origin of the Amish, and for him to revisit his old military base and the towns he saw almost forty years ago. I guess Ottie expected me to be happy and excited about his newest plans, but instead I almost choked. It took me off guard, like many times being with him did. Ottie has the gift to be pretty straightforward and overwhelming at times, something I for sure have not inherited from him. I feel bad about my reaction, and it is quite hard for me to explain. Maybe it is because it is still all pretty new. After all, I only knew him for about eleven months and I just need more time, but also I am more cautious because I learned with Edda. When you move things too fast it won't work out, especially if so many people are involved. I know it is so exciting for Ottie to have met me and Ross and the children, and for him, I am just an exciting addition for his family, but I already have a family, three actually; my husband and children, my mother and brother, and Edda and her family. I just managed, after almost nine years, to get the three of them in some sort of order, and now this will change the family dynamics all over again.

Come to think if it, I was actually really freaked out by the idea that Ottie wanted to go to Germany. Germany is my place, I do not know if I want to mix those two worlds any more than they are already. I do not want to make my mother feel uncomfortable. I want her to meet Ottie here, very casual, when she is here next time and she wants to, and then let her decide. If Ottie and Irene go to Germany I want it not to be awkward, but that they are welcome and have a good time. I also need to do my stuff there, meet my friends and family without them. I was also worried about my mother's feelings and her anticipation for us to come and visit her. I wanted her to have time to adjust to all those new developments first. On the other hand, I would really love for Irene to see the region I think her particular Amish group came from. I would like her to learn about German culture, and if she thinks it is similar to Amish. And Ottie, he should visit his old military base and the towns he knew, and maybe, even maybe, meet Edda. I do not know exactly, and I have to say writing it is almost scary, but maybe it would help Edda to finally get over the past and start a new life, and finally accept that this is a better solution. I did not know if she would want to meet him, but she might want to at some point. He would certainly like to, and Irene is very tolerant towards it, which I think is a really healthy way of thinking. She is a truly great woman.

My mother, in the meantime, was feeling better about me meeting Ottie. She had realized that our relationship had not changed at all with his appearance. Also, she told me, she was happy that especially now, I had someone more to take care of me and was there if I needed help. She even expressed the wish of meeting Ottie the next time she would come to visit us in the U.S. I was relieved to hear this, and told her about Ottie's travel plans. She did not seem to mind that either. I felt a little better now.

In the meantime, Ross's unemployment was very hard on all of us. We did not know that 2005 had one of the highest unemployment rates in years. Ross imagined he would write a few applications, get some interviews, and find a job pretty quickly. After all, his education was superior, and he had lots of actual job experiences from before and during his graduate work. But the 'real world' proved to be far more complicated. He had to write many applications, and many times he would never even hear back from the companies to which he sent them. He got really frustrated and felt useless at times. Being crowded in that little house did not help this feeling, and Ross was worried that our private health insurance would run out. We started questioning our decision to come to the Midwest. Should we have moved to Germany instead, where health insurance is socialized and you do not have to worry about your child getting sick? In addition, I could not work as much on my dissertation as I had planned, because Ross had to work much more on applications than he had planned, and could not help so much with watching Sean. To top it all off, my preliminary dissertation chapters were rejected by my committee, and I had to start all over again. In retrospect, my committee was right, but to see this at that moment was outright impossible. To share the one computer with Ross, and being cramped together all the time, was not promoting either of our ambitions. We had our first marriage quarrels. I wanted this thing to be over with so badly, and I wanted to leave this little house so much, I would have done anything.

But then, finally, in early December, a change was on the horizon. On a Friday morning, Ross found a job description from a company in Madison, our dream city, at Monster. Ross applied. Realizing that many companies did not react to applications from out-of-state, he used my cousin Andrea's address in Wisconsin. On Monday morning, Ross got a call, and the following Tuesday he went for an interview. We almost could not believe it... he got the job! The job was supposed to start in about four weeks, the beginning of January 2006. The only people who were a little sad about this development were my two mothers. They both hoped that Ross would find a job in Germany, where he sent many applications, but it seems that if you do not already live in the country, you have no chance of even being considered as a candidate.

We planned to go to Kentucky over the holidays, but before we left we started looking for a new house in Wisconsin. Andrea, my cousin, warmly recommended Oregon, a small 8,000-people village, just south of Madison, where she and her husband were living. It is a very child-friendly community, and so we focused our search to this area. After only looking at about twenty houses we found a beautiful home with a big yard and a brand new, large, dream kitchen! I was so ready to move, I think I would have almost moved anywhere. I persuaded Ross to make an offer. But before we could finalize the buy, Christmas came and we were on our way to Kentucky.

This time, the drive proved to be quite challenging with two little children and a dog. We had to take Xenon along, because of her age, combined with an extreme attachment to me and her recent anxiety attacks. Being left alone, even for a short amount of time, she would destroy windowsills, or doors, and being left outside she would dig a tunnel underneath the fence. We could not leave her with anybody, and I had started taking her with me in the car wherever I went. She even destroyed Carmen's seatbelt while we were looking at one of the houses. So that is why we took Xenon with us to Kentucky. Thank goodness for minivans, is all I can say! Ottie and Irene were really tolerant of Xenon in addition to their two little dogs, a white Maltese called Heidi, and a black Mapu called Schadde (a Pennsylvania Deutsch word for the German word "Schatten," meaning shadow). Xenon behaved surprisingly well considering the trip, but, after all, I was there with her and that was all that counted in her mind.

The kids were very excited to see Irene and Ottie. Ottie was on a diet, but for us he took a break from his program, and oh boy, do my relatives in Kentucky ever love to eat! Honestly, their food is good, but so heavy and caloric. When we came home after a week, we felt like eating only fruits and vegetables for several days. All this heavy food weighs you down and makes you tired and immobile.

Matthew has now lived with Ottie and Irene for three years, and I think he really is doing well. He got his GED and started college, even though he almost never went to school. He tried to earn his own money to support his car and personnel expenses. He is really funny and loves to talk, sometimes a little too much, but that is okay. I think Matthew will make his way.

For Samantha, on the other hand, I am a little more worried. I went out with her alone one day, because I wanted to get to know her a little better, and without other people around. We had some nice conversations. She told me she was intimidated by me and Ross at first, because we are so highly educated. I am the perfect daughter in her mind, a scientist and married to a scientist. How strange, I never felt different, but here we are, treated like something special, it almost seemed like playing a role to me. I would like for Samantha to see me as a friend. I do not know if this is possible, since I am twenty years older. Samantha is kind of rebellious, and in desperate need of finding herself. I hope she will someday.

I had some time to spend with Monte as well, and I really enjoyed that. It is funny; we actually kept finding more and more similarities. We read similar books and like the same TV shows, like *Star Trek, The Next Generation*, we both have and love our cats, and have a liking for the renaissance. On our way home from Kentucky, we stopped at Monte's hometown and met his mother and stepfather. His mother Frankie is only eleven years older than me, and a tiny person. Like Monte, she had red hair. Her eyes twinkle, but you can see in her stature that despite her petite appearance she was used to physically work hard in her life. Her husband is tall, even taller than Monte. He had grey thick hair and like Frankie, one can tell that he is used to physical labor. He is a pipe fitter like Monte, and often he is Monte's boss. I think they like to work together, and you can see that there is mutual respect between the two men. They were a very nice couple, Frankie and Bob, and to our surprise they had pictures of us all over their house. It is interesting in how many homes there are pictures of us, and especially our children. We play such an important role in so many lives, that it is sometimes almost surreal.

I think both Ottie and Frankie hoped that I could somehow become some sort of a real sister to Monte. That was not unfamiliar to me since that was also what Edda had wanted me to be for Amelie. It is very honoring to me, and I hope I can somehow meet their expectations. I learned, however, through my previous experiences with my three sisters, that those things do not come naturally, and it requires lots of work and time to establish a real, honest relationship that has the power to live through harder times. With Amelie, and my other two sisters, I think we had established a relationship that was not the same as one found between siblings who had grown up together, but we lived through some troubled times and our relationships had survived. We somehow grew together. Maybe that is what real relationships need, growing together, living through difficult times with various problems to establish a unique relationship with every person you know, be it your partner, friend, or sibling.

CHAPTER 17

Beyond the Cheddar Curtain

In February of 2006, to be exact, February 18, we moved beyond the "Cheddar Curtain," as people from Illinois so lovingly call the border of Wisconsin. I was so happy. Monte even came to stay with us for some days and help us. And I have to say, without him, it would have been more challenging to move. He is very strong. We moved on a Saturday at twenty degrees Fahrenheit below zero, and high snow in Wisconsin. Some nice neighbor had shoveled the driveway so we could drive the moving truck in. Only six weeks later I found out who it was, when the snow finally receded and we could go outside and meet neighbors. Our new house was beautiful; the 2800 square feet seemed like a castle to us, and the kitchen was just to die for: big, new with an attached dining area. There was a patio door to the outside deck. The house was a tri-level; the entrance door and the garage, however, were the only things on the middle, street level. When you come in you can either go half a story up or down. The downstairs was half outside the ground in the front of the house and completely out of the ground in the back of the house. Going up the stairs, you entered the nice big living room to your left. Across from the stairs was a big opening to the dining area of the kitchen. The kitchen itself is basically behind the living room. The cabinets are cherry color with a contemporary look and without ornamental decoration, just as we like it: simple and straight. To the right of the stairs there was a hallway leading to the three bedrooms and the bathroom. The master bedroom, which has two big closets, has its own small, but well-designed bathroom, with a walk-in shower with glass doors. What a dream after the cramped little pink bathroom with the constant draft in the middle of winter.

Downstairs was a big family room with a patio door leading outside to the huge yard. There is a small laundry room, a guest bathroom, a storage room with the furnace in it and two small bedrooms. It seemed like the perfect house and we did not even have enough furniture to fill it all. What a dream come true! The neighborhood was about thirty years old, with large trees and people who had lived there for a long time. I really liked this. We became very good friends with all of our neighbors.

Monte stayed with us for three days. That is nice, and we actually spent some time together alone. Monday we went shopping for a dryer. Sean was with us while Ross was at work and Carmen in school. I think Monte liked it with us. We had time to talk about his story and of his parents before and after the divorce when he was still a small child.

In May 2006, my mother and my Aunt Dorle, Andrea's mother, came to visit. In our new home we had enough space to accommodate lots of visitors, and my mother would have her own bedroom downstairs. Aunt Dorle would stay with my cousin, of course. The weather was beautiful, the winter had ended as fast as it had come. I picked my mother up at the airport and drove the twenty minutes to our house. My mother really liked our new home, and was very happy for us. She and my aunt had so much fun. My cousin Andrea had to work, so every morning at around nine she would bring her mother over to our house, or my mother and I would pick her up later during the day for trips around Wisconsin. Every afternoon we had coffee and homemade cake and Derek, Andrea's husband would come to join. He did not speak any German, but he had lots of fun, seeing the three of us talking and gesturing. Even my cousin, Thomas, from St. Paul, came to visit for a few days to see his aunts. He had not seen them in quite a while, and it was a wonderful family reunion. I love my family, and having them all in Wisconsin was absolutely wonderful. It was Carmen's birthday, and the weather was so nice we could even celebrate outside.

And then, guess what, shortly before my mother and aunt left again, Ottie came on a short trip to meet them! Can you believe it? Clearly, that day was one of the most emotional days I have had in a long time. Ottie planned he and Irene's book-signing tour so they could stop by here and visit a day before my mother would fly home. It was really important to me that they meet, but I was very nervous nevertheless. My mother and I baked cake and cooked dinner, German hamburgers with onions and peppers and breadcrumbs and spices. Irene planned to give a talk at the Oregon Library about growing up Amish, and our kids would be dressed up as little Amish children.

I knew Ottie was really nervous about meeting my mother. He called a day before to ask how to address my mother. In Germany, the polite form to address an adult is "Herr" (Mr.) or "Frau" (Mrs.) using their last name. My mother, however, knows how the customs are in the U.S., and since through me they were kind of related, she told me to tell him to call her Jane, which is short for her real name Christiane.

Then, finally during the afternoon, Irene and Ottie arrived. My mother and I went outside to the car to greet them. We all, my mother, Irene, Ottie and I, sat down at the table. It was then that Ottie started to talk. He told my mother that he did not want to excuse what he had done, but that he had been young and foolish and if he could change the past, he would. He continued that he was so grateful for the loving and caring home I had through my wonderful parents, who had raised me to become a compassionate and respectful and loving person. Tears filled my eyes and I could barely keep from crying out loud. I admired Ottie for his strength to say all this, although I knew how nervous he was at the same time. But also, it made me kind of uncomfortable to hear this about myself. Of course, everybody likes to hear good things about themselves but this was a little too much. I do have faults as well. I actually needed to leave the room when they told each other what a wonderful person I was and how proud they were of me. It was almost more than I could take. I guess, somehow, when I tell my story, it is almost as if I talk about somebody else, but then, when it is clearly me, I can barely take it.

Ottie later told me that he thinks that everything happens for a reason, and I definitely believe this to be true. I believe in my heart that it was meant for me to grow up with my parents and not my birth parents. It made me who I am today, not just growing up, but also the experience of meeting my birth parents and my siblings. Ottie also told me that he would have liked to meet my father as well. That made me choke up again. I always get really emotional when my father is mentioned, and it meant a lot to me that Ottie considered my late father as well. Ottie told me that if my father was just half as nice as my mother, he would have been a wonderful person. I think it was very important that Ottie and my mother met, because it made Ottie more aware that I did have another family, a family who loves me and where I belong. My mother, on the other hand, told Ottie how grateful she and my father were to have been my parents, and how blessed they were. I really tried to keep from crying, but it was almost impossible it was so emotional. Then, when they were more acquainted with each other, they actually started comparing characteristics I had inherited from either Ottie or Edda. Oh my goodness, I felt between uncomfortable and amused. Again, it almost felt as if they were talking about somebody else rather than me. I can barely explain the feelings I had sitting there with them, hearing them talk together. The happiness I felt and the relief and almost disbelief that this was really happening.

Later on my cousin, Andrea, her husband Derek, and my aunt came over. My aunt was immediately smitten with Ottie. I could not believe it. Even my cousin confirmed that Ottie was indeed a charmer. They loved Irene and Ottie instantly, and later on told me what a really cool guy Ottie was, and how awesome this all was. Boy, were they right. It was almost like being in a dream or watching a cheesy soap opera. Ottie told my mother that although he was thrilled – I think that is his favorite word, next to tickled – to have met me, he knew that she was my mother and that my father was my father, and that he only hoped to become a good family friend. Okay, if I had not cried before, now certainly was the time. I did not know how much of this I could bear. I was so proud of my mother and Ottie and so grateful for all my life and this event. I was so grateful that my mother was so cool and got along with both of my birth parents so well.

I was in such a positive mood that I finally knitted the jacket I promised Edda so many years earlier. Yes, I know, you may think I did this because I felt bad, but to the contrary. I was just so relieved and I have to say, even though I used to knit so much when I was younger, I had not knitted in a long time and all this stress prevented me from being in the right mood. But now was the time. I used a very soft Alpaca yarn, which a friend brought me from Peru, and because of that it was very special to me. Edda was so happy, and loved its light weight, and Karl was pleased with the brownish color. Some day though, I will make her a bright colored sweater!

Edda wanted to come and visit again for a long time, but Karl no longer wanted to fly. Finally, in June, Sophie called and told me that she and Edda would come together to visit in September. I cannot express how happy I was about this news. First of all, I was glad that Sophie had called. I had been warned in the beginning that it would be hard to get close to Sophie. I had my arguments with all three of them, but usually with Amelie and Christine, we would simply talk it out, but with Sophie I did not know how to approach things. I assume because of her own illness, she was not always in the mood to communicate, and it was hard for me to keep up with our relationship. I was always so happy when she called, and that she and Edda would come together seemed like a wonderful idea.

A few weeks later, during one of my weekly calls with my mother, she told me that Edda had visited her by herself that day. They looked at old photo albums and watched the videotapes of the time my mother had been visiting just a few weeks earlier. My mother told me that Edda was a very nice woman, and how much more open and more relaxed she was visiting without her husband. They even looked at the pictures of Ottie and Irene and my mother said that Edda took it very well. Edda told my mother that she did not feel anything looking at them, that he had died for her when he left her and me. But I think that that is not true. I think she really loved him very much, and wished everything had been different. She also told my mother that I had told Edda she was better off having not married him. I still believe this to be the truth; he was just too young.

At the end of July 2006, we went to Kentucky during the summer vacation. In fact, the kids and I, along with Monte, went to visit the Garretts. Ross had to work and could not take any time off from the corporate American company, so Monte and I decided that I would drive the six hours to Indiana and then he would drive the rest to Kentucky. Monte prepared lunch for us when we arrived at his house, and after some time for the kids to run around his yard and play with his cat, we continued our trip. The five hours he drove went as fast as lightning, and we basically talked with each other the whole time. It was really great going on vacation with Monte. He was very good to the kids, and I think he would be a wonderful father. He learned quickly how to buckle their seatbelts properly, and wanted detailed instructions on how to use an *Epipen* after he learned that I carried one around for my food allergies. Monte was a really great companion; for example when Ottie and Irene slept during the day after a night of card games, he took us to a lake. I was so glad that he was there. Matthew was in his room most of the day, and Samantha did not really spend much time with us. The four of us went to the movies together, but that was about it. Sam and I went out for lunch and had a good talk, but I guess there is a generation between us and after all, I am almost as old as her mother.

It had been Ottie's wish to perform a DNA test. Despite the fact that he wanted to do one, he was hoping that I could get

American citizenship once his fatherhood was proven. The day we went to get our blood drawn Ottie seemed different and strange, I think he was actually nervous. He told me that there was no reason not to believe that I was his child, especially when looking at Sean, but maybe he was scared. He likes us, me, Ross, and the kids and I knew that even if the test would be negative we would stay part of his family. I felt though, that by being scared of the result of the test, he distrusted Edda and that was not good. On the other hand, it had been so long ago and I understood a little uneasiness on his part. Ottie came to love us, and he did not want to lose that.

Some weeks later, we got the results and they said that "to 99.7% he cannot be excluded as my biological father," which is lawyer talk for a positive result. Ottie was relieved, but wanted me to interpret all the numbers on the result paper. When I talked to Frankie, Monte's mother, a few days later, she suddenly also inquired about the results. When I told her, she said,

"I am so glad!"

I think she was just very happy for Monte, who had grown to like his new sister, brother-in-law and niece and nephew. I think that really meant a lot to Frankie, to have a sibling for Monte, a sibling his age. Frankie is a very kind person, kind of quiet and I like her an awful lot. It is funny to think that she is not that much older than Ross and me in the grand scheme of things, only eleven years older than me and nine older than Ross. When I later talked to Monte I said:

"Well, you cannot get rid of me now. I am officially your sister."

He seemed to be genuinely happy and said that it would have not mattered to him anyway. That was nice of him to say. It was a strange feeling, for some reason it did make me happy that I was officially related to them all. Although I had not been nervous while taking the test, I seemed to be relieved that the results were positive. I was pleased and honored to be accepted and loved by so many people, and that was the most important thing.

CHAPTER 18

When the Past and the Future Merge

At the end of August 2006, Edda and Sophie came to visit us in Oregon, Wisconsin. I was so excited. I was very pleased about the two of them coming together. It would mean I could freely talk to Edda and I could get to know Sophie better. Like my mother, they arrived at the Madison airport, where I picked them up. On the way home, I could tell how excited they were. We had a guest room set downstairs for the two of them. The kids were already sleeping when they arrived, but they were very excited to see them in the morning. As soon as Carmen and Sean woke up they sneaked down to the guest room and knocked carefully on the door. This would become a morning ritual, and every morning the kids would pretend to wake up Oma Edda and Sophie.

We had a great time. It seemed that Sophie and I, for the first time, really connected, and felt relaxed with each other. Sophie told me that, for most of her life, she had been in pain from her arthritis, and that made her shelter herself from most people. Sophie had a blast in the U.S. She loved it here, loved the openness and friendliness of the people and how much more relaxed everybody is than in Germany. Yes, Germans can be a little complicated at times, and that at a grocery store the cashier asked with a smile "How are you today?" and "Did you find everything?" is unheard of in Germany, where most of the time you feel like a burden rather than a customer.

I was relieved that this time Karl did not come, and Edda and I could finally openly and at length talk about Ottie and my third family. At times though, it still felt strange, as if I was talking about somebody else and not that I was actually, in a way, the center of this story. Many times too, I needed to keep myself emotionally detached from the whole story. On one side, I feel so much for Edda and on the other side, I feel like I am betraying my own family, my parents, and my brother.

It is so immensely sad when Edda tells me about the time right after my birth when the nurses took me away. Edda told me how she would sneak into the nursery at night and that there was a compassionate nurse who would, against the law, give me to her to hold. She told me how she had so much milk and nobody to nurse and that later on she had no milk for her other daughters, and she felt as if it was a punishment because she had given me away.

Ottie decided to write Edda a letter and apologize for his behavior, and to explain to her how everything happened. He worked very long on this letter, and knowing that he could not send it to Edda personally, sent it to me to give to her when she was visiting. He read parts to me while writing it, and this time it was I who became emotional, and I had to cry. I was hoping so much that the letter would help Edda to close the past, and finally have some answers and maybe some relief. Ottie wanted to come see her in person, but Edda was not ready for this, at least not yet. So, finally, after Sophie and Edda had been there for a few days, I gave Edda the letter. She took it, but waited some time before trying to read it. Then she and Sophie tried to read it, but did not understand it all, so finally I took the letter and we all sat on our balcony with coffee and cake, of course, and I translated the letter:

Dear Edda,

I have spent the last year-and-a-half trying to find the right words to explain to you what happened almost forty years ago. Then, I realized there are really no words to express my emotions about finding out we share a daughter. My heart is happy, because of Julia and how well her life has turned out, but heavy with sad-

ness because of what you must have endured having to make such a difficult choice in your life. I can try to explain what happened and hope it might give you some peace. I am truly regretful for any and all the pain I unknowingly put you through and hope you can find it in your heart to forgive me.

It's been a long time ago and I remember how happy we both were when you told me we were going to have a child. I asked my commanding officer for permission to marry and was told I had to ask the Army chaplain and several others in order to get permission. After weeks of talks and requests, I was denied permission and was no longer allowed off base. I was angry and asked to be discharged, but at eighteen years of age, it too was denied. The next thing I knew, I was being shipped back state-side without a chance to talk to you. I was told many lies and I believed each and every one, but even so I should have been stronger. I can understand if you can't forgive me but I only hope you can try to understand if possible.

You have nothing to be ashamed of and you were very brave to do what you did. I'm sorry I was not as strong as you. Julia has given you and me two beautiful grandchildren and we can be so proud of everything she has accomplished. She has your strength and courage. God works in ways that are sometimes hard to understand, but I believe he had angels caring and watching over Julia and her adoptive parents. They have given Julia so many things you and I may not have been able to. Most of all they loved her and gave her a wonderful childhood. Julia has touched so many lives and I am sure each person is better off because of her. I know I am!

I can remember a special time in my life when I was young and strong and the world was beautiful and exciting and you, Edda were part of my life. You will always be a part of my life and Julia is a reminder of that time. May God always bless you and keep you safe from harm.

Sincerely,
Ottie A. Garrett

We all were close to tears, but we all tried to be strong and not let the emotions show too much. Oh, how I was hoping that this letter would help Edda a little bit, but of course, as Ottie had put it, there was nothing anyone could do to give her the time back and nothing one could say to her to comfort her for the time she lost with me. Why we cannot really show our emotions in front of each other I really cannot say. Maybe we do not feel comfortable enough with each other, maybe we are not ready yet to show each other our weaknesses. It is so hard, she is my mother and yet, she is not. I feel sad, but only for her and that is even sadder. It seems that she is the only one in this story who actually suffered and who can never be given back what she lost. Ottie gained a daughter, a son-in-law, and grandchildren, I gained a mother, a father, tons of siblings, a grandfather and step-grandmother, aunts and uncles, but Edda, since she cannot even say who we are, did not really get us back. Because as it were, even though moving and meeting totally new people, her husband, in the end, could not get over the shadow of letting people know about me and my heritage. And so we stayed some distant relatives from America and our pictures remained hidden in boxes.

After the first emotional time was passed and we had digested the right amount of German cheesecake and coffee, Edda told me to tell Ottie that she was glad about the letter, but could not really forgive him or forget the past. At least the beginning was done and maybe some sort of closure was received. When Edda and Sophie left, Ottie basically called immediately afterwards. He was not allowed to call during the time they were here. I told him on the phone about my birth and how I was taken away and how she had sneaked into the nursery and was sometimes able to hold me for a few minutes. At this point, Ottie actually had to hang up the phone because he got so emotional, and call me back some time later on to finish the conversation. He told me:

"This makes me very sad right now."

And I answered: "Yes, it should."

I felt that Edda should not be the only one to suffer a little bit of that emotion, and he should have to experience all those feelings, too. I was not angry at him, but I thought that it was okay for him to feel a little of the pain she felt and all that she had to go through before and after I had come back.

At the same time the political situation in the U.S. started to worsen. The war had cost many lives of our soldiers and innocent civilians of both countries. During the midst of all this, I had called Ottie one day and was cut short, because a recruiter was visiting.

"A recruiter?" I asked, "For whom?"

"Samantha," he answered.

Did he not know that he was sending her into her own death?

"Oh, no," he said, "they won't send her overseas, and also, women do not fight in combat."

Then he hung up. I felt anger and hatred at the same time. In fact I was furious! I called Monte and had to leave a message because he was not there. I was panicked and stammered in broken English – I seem to not be able to speak proper English when I am furious – that he should persuade Sam – who loves Monte and does pretty much everything he tells her – to not become a soldier. It would surely kill her, because lots of people were not killed in combat but just by roadside bombs or other attacks. And even if she did not get killed, she would see such unbelievable things of horror that she would never be the same person again. I did not want that to happen to her.

Monte did not call back for three days, during which time I talked to Ottie and Irene several times. Although we like each other, we have the extreme opposite political opinions and we can argue forever. When Monte finally called back, he told me that Sam was there with him. She wanted a few days to decide and had gone to visit Monte. And, since he could not really tell her the message I had left, he had saved it for her and played it for her.

"She really cares for me," was her response, and she did

not sign up for the army! I was so relieved and in disbelief at the same time. She did not go because of me. I had made a difference! Ottie was angry and he said that Sam had called me a hippie, but he thought I was a flower girl. I saw that as a compliment. It was an uplifting experience. I like being called a hippie or flower girl. I had always thought I should have been born twenty years earlier. But maybe I can still change some things and make the world a better place.

In January of 2007, I decided that, finally, this had to be the year I was finishing my dissertation. So many things had happened, but my ten years were up and I had to finish. It was now or never. My committee was extremely patient with me and supportive. They believed in me even if I did not. I planned a trip to Tucson in April, first to defend my dissertation, but when this was not working out, I would at least fly and talk to my committee. I had decided to bring Carmen along because I had promised her to visit Tucson at least one more time, so she could see her old friends, the little people she spent a wonderful early childhood with. We had a great time, as it was a time just for me and Carmen. I was surprised though, how little Carmen remembered at first. Even our old house she almost did not remember. However, to her defense, it had changed quite a bit with wooden walls added on the outside and apparently on the inside also. Too bad, it was such a beautiful house.

My sister, Christine, finally fulfilled her dream and moved to Bosnia to find a permanent job. In the beginning, it was not so easy, and she lost three jobs in a row and had difficulties getting a work permit. In the meantime, her father was diagnosed with mesophilioma, a rare form of lung cancer, which is caused by asbestos exposure. Karl was a building constructor and must have gotten into contact with asbestos many years ago, most likely while working in Frankfurt. It usually takes around forty years to develop, and his days were numbered. The doctors told him he had three months and he should have lung surgery. He has asthma, and the idea of taking away part of his lung was impossible for him. He decided against the operation, and started taking homeopathic medicines and several rounds of chemotherapy. Karl seemed to respond surprisingly well to the chemo, and although he was getting weaker and thinner from the therapy, he started believing in life again.

At the end of August, the day finally came, and I went to Tucson, alone this time, to defend my dissertation. What I should tell you is that it was actually really good. I did a good job, the presentation was professional and I was not nervous at all. That was it? That was what I had been dreading for ten years? It was over and I could not believe it. And guess what, I got depressed. My whole life I had been a student, I had identified myself with being a student, and what was I, a homemaker? Nothing against that, but I felt suddenly lonely and not belonging to anything anymore. It was the strangest feeling, and it took me almost eight months to get over it. Next year, around that time, when Sean will go to kindergarten and I finally will have more time, maybe I can work part-time as an archaeologist. Time will tell.

Karl spontaneously told me on the phone, when I called to tell the good news, that he would invite all of us to a restaurant when we came to visit the next time. I think he was proud of me. I was really getting accustomed to him, talking to him now on the phone so many times, and discussing his health and his feelings. That was a big relief for me.

Although I had always stated that the only reason to finish was to wear the regalia and walk in the graduation ceremony, I decided that flying to Tucson a third time that year would be too costly, and just too much stress all together. Finding a house sitter, and someone to take care of the kids while Ross and I were in Tucson was not easy. I decided instead, as a gift to myself for finishing my Ph.D., to fly to Germany all by myself for my twenty-year high school reunion and my godchild, Anna's confirmation. Both events were luckily just one week apart. Since my trip fell on Thanksgiving, Ross could easily take off work that week and have some valuable father-children time.

As always, things did not go as planned. It started when I called Ottie to tell him that I was going to Germany.

"Do you want some company?" he asked.

Well, that was not exactly what I had planned. Carefully, I asked what he meant. He explained to me once more, that it was Irene's greatest wish to see Germany, the country of her heritage.

"Do you mind taking her along on your trip?"

I told him that I had to ask my mother about this first, after all, Irene should stay with me during this time. It was a strange prospect taking my young "stepmother" with me to Germany to live with my mother, and meet my entire family and most of my friends. You have to know my trips to Germany go like this: in the morning see a friend, in the afternoon have coffee and cake with another friend, and if there is still some time I have dinner with yet another friend. Then there is my family, who was looking forward to seeing me and who I dearly love, and my birth mother and her husband. How would I manage to see Edda without Karl knowing who Irene was? A very complicated and iffy situation, which involved careful consideration of all the aspects and people involved.

Finally, I decided to call my mother. After all, it was her house Irene would be staying, and her time with me she would be shared. It did not take her a long time to decide. My mother really liked Irene from the time she met her in our house, and since it would only be a little more than a week, only me visiting, and she had an extra bedroom, she invited Irene to come along. Oh, what a wonderful mother I have!

Ottie was ecstatic, and so was Irene. I booked the flights and it was set. Irene had to take a flight from Nashville to Chicago, where she and I met and then we would fly together the 8.5 hours straight to Frankfurt. We booked the flight in June for November, and I think after a while Ottie had some second thoughts about letting his wife leave for "so long." One time he called me to ask if I should maybe take Monte instead, since he really wanted Irene and himself to go together at a later time. Ottie and Irene had never, in their eleven years of marriage, been separated for more than a day or two. I informed Ottie that a ticket could not be changed to another person's name, and that Monte also would get his turn in coming with me to Germany. Irene would be fine and so would Ottie. The closer the time got, the more Irene and I spent on the phone planning our trip, finding presents for my mother, brother, and other people we might be staying with or visiting. I started rearranging my visiting plans accommodating Irene and her yearning to see different places, but at the same time visiting the most important friends and family. Did I mention that I love to plan? I make plans months in advance, changing them, working on them, adjusting them, and finally calling everybody and confirming my schedule. I can tell you, and Ross reminded me to mention that he will affirm this, to travel with me is not as easy as it sounds. I live for visiting people. What many do not understand is that I do not get to go to Germany that often, and if I do, well, I need to make the most of it. I love my family and friends and I want to see them all.

Finally, I came to an agreeable conclusion on what to do during our trip to make it my present, and at the same time memorable for Irene. And then it was time to go. When I was younger – wow, I never thought I would say this – I used to fly around the world several times a year. Today, I like flying less and less. Not that I hate it or fear it, it is just that I do not enjoy it anymore. The sitting in a small space for a long time, waiting for food, which then does not taste at all like the "continental gourmet dinner" that had been promised, waiting in line for a tiny bathroom, flooded with who knows what, and drinking tomato juice, which under normal circumstances I would not even touch. Oh well, if I want to get somewhere I will have to take the plane.

Then I had to decide on another issue: Edda. Of course I wanted to see her, but what would I do about Irene? How should I tell Edda that I was bringing Ottie's wife along with me to Germany? And what about Karl? He could not know who Irene was. Not that I understand that whole issue, but that is just how it is, and is it my place to judge other people's relationships and decisions? As long as it does not hurt me, or my family, everybody has to decide how they deal with certain issues in life. Well, I decided to let Edda know that Irene was coming. I was a little afraid that Edda would be sad, thinking maybe I had a better relationship with Ottie than with her. That, of course, was ridiculous. Every relationship is unique and not comparable. And also, maybe Edda did not think anything of it, in which case I was silly to even have thoughts like this. Anyway, again, things worked out very different than expected.

After I told Edda on the phone that Irene was coming, she wrote me a letter (she cannot say those things on the phone, since Karl would hear them) saying that she wanted to meet Irene, if she would agree to that. Well, that I had not expected. My first thought was, "Why would she want that?"

But then I thought about it, and decided that it was probably not such a bad idea, and might help Edda to acknowledge the situation today and realize that the past is no longer present, and that Ottie had a new life, just as she did. Of course that whole issue had me change my visitation plans again, since now not only did I have to plan a visit with Edda and Karl by myself, but also a secret meeting with Edda and Irene! As I mentioned before though, I am a planning expert and so it was all accomplished.

While I was in Germany, Ross, the kids, and Vargus were planning on going to Kentucky to make our famous Thanksgiving dinner at Ottie's house. Monte also planned to come, and so it would be the first Thanksgiving in eleven years that I would miss.

I chose the night flight, in hopes that we could get a little sleep on the plane. Irene was already at the airport in Chicago when I arrived on the bus, the expected three hours before schedule. Check-in was easy and fast and so we met at the gate. Irene had never flown internationally before, but I knew the airport and its accommodations blindfolded. We had some dinner and waited. There was a lot to talk about though, and even pictures to take: Irene in front of the gate, the sign with "Frankfurt" on it, Irene in the airplane and so on. We even did some last minute duty-free shopping. Then it was time to board. And guess what, we were even able to sleep for five hours. I am telling you, the night flights are the best.

In Frankfurt, we had to go through immigration and customs. Immigration is so much easier than in America, and does not take long at all in Frankfurt: one of the biggest airports in Europe. Our luggage came relatively fast, and since there was nobody at customs, we were free to go. My brother was waiting outside the gate and warmly greeted Irene. He had never met her before, but through photographs, videotapes, and my mother's narratives, she did not seem unfamiliar to him. My brother had lost some weight and he looked great. It was Friday morning, and the airport was relatively empty. Of course my brother had parked his car, like usual, at the other end of Terminal 1, so we had to walk underneath the entire terminal to get to the parking garage.

Irene got a first impression of the necessities of bakeries at every corner. Oh, the wonders of German pastries and bread, which is one of the things I miss the most on the other side of the big ocean. I love bread, good bread, heavy bread with grains and crust and flavor, and pastries with hazelnuts, and chocolate made with hazelnuts. Have I ever mentioned the fact that Germans cannot live without hazelnuts and the wonders of Nutella and of course Hanuta, chocolate delights made out of hazelnuts? My husband does not like hazelnuts, or anything made out of them, and his range of pastries shrinks quite a bit as a result. "Germans and hazelnuts," he will say shaking his head, when he finds yet another product with the heavenly delight.

Finally, we found Christopher's car, which, to Irene's astonishment, is not much bigger that a shoe box. Irene learned quickly on the half-hour trip to my hometown all about a German "Autobahn." My brother likes to drive fast. And I mean fast. What does, let's say, 150 or 160 km/hour mean to you? Fast? Oh yes, that is fast, around 120 miles per hour fast! And he drives that fast even though most of the Autobahns today do have speed limits ranging from 100 to 130 km/hour, which translate to 65 to 85 miles per hour.

We finally arrived in my hometown. Gau-Algesheim is a very old and proud little town with little streets that have not changed in size since the 1200s. Some of the houses are over 400 years old, and some of the defensive wall built in the twelfth century is still standing. Gau-Algesheim was first mentioned in the 600s, and people are happy and proud to live here. Family names go back through the centuries. Although Gau-Algesheim has become a commuter town for Frankfurt and Mainz, it has kept its ambience. The town never really grew too much, even though we have some newer developments from the 70s and the 80s. It is now expensive to live here, a result of the good infrastructure caused by the train tracks going to Frankfurt. Irene could not believe how narrow the streets are, and how relatively fast we drive through them, seemingly paying no attention to the cars parked in the streets, which make them even more constricted. We passed by the church, located in the center of town, with a beautifully designed plaza area and some stores grouped around it. It was noon, and the stores were closed. Yes, they are closed on a Friday. In Germany, stores close around noon for about two hours. Then they reopen. Our two banks, however, are closed for the weekend, something I had not thought about when we passed the exchange booths at the airport. I had to lend Irene some German money for the weekend.

As always, seeing my mother after a long time, is really emotional. My mother just had a knee replacement six weeks prior, but was doing amazingly fine. She was so excited to have me there, and almost alone. Being a mother myself, I understand. For ten years now, I had not come alone but in the company of others. Although she loves and respects my husband and loves her grandchildren, it is different than having my undivided attention. Irene, as we realize pretty soon, is not really an intrusion, but rather very nice company. She was very attentive to my mother, helped clean up, brought her a chair to put her leg on, and was an absolute perfect and pleasant guest.

My mother prepared a light lunch and we all, my brother included, sat at the kitchen table and ate. We had a pleasant meal with interesting conversation. After cleaning the kitchen, we decided to go for a little walk. Along the way we had the opportunity to catch sight of some of the old wineries, which are hidden all over within the town. From the outside these old farms look like average old houses, but when you get a glance inside one of their courtyards, you see how big they are hidden behind the old walls. We walked along stores on the narrow sidewalk, which barely fits one person.

We continued walking to the left, and passed in front of the beautiful, gothic church, the foundation placed down in the 6th century. The church is a special place here in town. Its tower is the highest building, and its bell rings every fifteen minutes, that is, if there is not another reason to ring, let's say for a wedding, a birth, a death, or any other reason you might imagine. I never realized how much the bells ring until Irene told me that when you cannot sleep, you hear them all the time and can count the minutes and the hours. The bells can be heard all over town, and personally, I miss them here in Wisconsin. We took pictures in front of the church. It is a Catholic church, and basically everybody in town is Catholic. The church is a central part of town, not only architecturally, but also as a focal point of the social life. The church organizes the local youth groups, the volunteer work at the local elderly home, and the visitation group for Gau-Algesheimers who are hospitalized in the bigger towns in the vicinity, just to name a few.

We walked along the church to the local cemetery. It was nice to walk through the old, wooded cemetery between the big, monumental gravestones showing the history of the families in town. Every grave is nicely decorated with flowers and trees and big engraved gravestones. Little stone walls encircle each individual or family grave. My mother takes good care of my father's grave. It had been nine years since my father died. Irene took a picture of us at the grave, something we had never done, but somehow it is nice she did it. It is not as strange as I thought to see those pictures after the fact. Personally, I do not connect this grave with my father. I would rather remember him in other ways, in photographs, tapes, and his old diary about the Second World War.

Then we walked the last steep part of the hill back to our house. Although she only had her new knee for six weeks, my mother was doing very well with walking, as long as we walk slower than normal and support her a little when walking uphill. At home, we made coffee and ate the real German cheesecake; not the German cheesecakes you can buy in American bakeries but the real one with real "quark," a milk product Germans love to put on bread, use for dessert, and to make cheesecakes. It was my wish to have this for coffee. But let me tell you about Germans and having coffee. In the afternoon, Germans love to have their coffee and cake; kind of like the British have their "tea time." Sometimes, neighbors or friends come over and we have coffee and cake together. If you meet another German in America, almost the first thing you do is to invite them for coffee and cake.

The next day we had a full schedule. In the morning, we walked through town again and visited my Bärbel and her daughter Anna, my godchild. Anna was one of the reasons I came to Germany this time. She was to be confirmed in the Catholic Church, and I would be there with her. It was an honor for me, more maybe than she can imagine. Anna is the sweetest girl you can imagine, always eager to help, kind, good-mannered, and open-minded. She loves languages, and is quite good at learning them. Anna and I have developed a very close relationship over the years. She even came to visit us in Tucson one year when she was just fourteen. Now, she is a grown woman, working in her apprenticeship and getting confirmed.

After that, we visited my friend Gülay, who cut my hair and tried to "style" it as well as possible, with me trying to fight every single make-up or hair product she tried to use. She insisted I should wear a skirt for my reunion that evening, and asked Irene to make sure I would do so. That night, I left Irene with my mother and went with Heike to our twenty-year high school reunion. It was fun. About 40 of the original 74 women (I went to a Catholic Nuns school for girls, no laughing please) came. Heike and I met with Anne and Andrea, two of our group of friends for over thirty years! Astrid, unfortunately, could not come, since she was living in Switzerland at that time, and was expecting her second child two days later. Anne was also expecting her second daughter, but since she lived close by, she came. It was funny to try to remember names of the women coming into the rooms. After two hours though, the faces seemed familiar again and we could remember more and more. It was a simple and fun reunion, no fancy event. We just had fun eating dinner at a local restaurant, which is owned by one of our former class.

After sleeping in a little (I did not fall asleep before 2 a.m., again), I had breakfast with my mother and Irene. Later on that morning, Heike came to pick us up. She and Stefan had just bought an old house near Heidelberg. I was the first of our "clique," my group of best friends, to see this house. I was proud of that. I live so far away and I still managed to be the first to see this beautiful little house. We went to see Heidelberg first. Heidelberg is a very picturesque town, known for its very famous, enormous, and abosolutley beautiful "Heidelberger Schloss," a very famous and enormous castle ruin. However, poor Irene could not enjoy the walk through town and the castle so much, since she was almost obsessed with buying "the perfect gift" for the entire Garrett clan. I almost felt bad for her. The first hit came when she discovered that, in Germany, basically all stores are closed on Sundays; and it was Sunday. The only open stores we found were somewhat cheesy tourist traps. The second blow came when Heike and

I tried to convince Irene that Germans do not, I repeat, do not hang Christmas ornaments saying "Germany" on them on their Christmas trees, ergo there are no such things to buy. The third problem was that a "typical" German the "Bierstein," the heavy, decorated ceramic beer glass with a handle, is not seen as we are from the wine area of Germany. In our hometowns, we drink wine. You can buy wine glasses and containers, but not necessarily beer glasses. Also, the praised "Kuckucksuhr," the cuckoo clock, comes from a region called "Schwarzwald," the black forest, and if you can find one of those clocks in other places you might really want to check its authenticity.

Well, believe it or not, Irene finally found a tourist store with beer glasses, "Trachtenpuppen" (dolls with traditional German clothing), "Kuckucksuhren," and all other things a tourist might see as "real" German. I have to admit, even I found a "Pyramide," a wooden candle chime, depicting the nativity scene, which turns when the candles are lit. This artifact, which I had admired at friends' houses during my childhood, is beautifully crafted with little detailed wooden ornaments. Heike bought it for me for Christmas.

Now, heavily loaded, we walked back to the car and continued our hair-raising trip with Heike to her new home. Their house, a 100 + year hunting house originally built by a baroness, is small but beautifully remodeled. Its first story resembles the style of an old castle, with its rounded wooded entry door and rock cornerstones. It has three stories, but is altogether only about 1000 square foot. Heike and Stefan, although they had just moved in a few weeks earlier, have decorated the house in their unique style using artifacts gathered from their numerous trips all over the world, including South America, many countries in Africa, and Asia. Stefan is an excellent cook and created a wonderful dinner, and with the help of Amarula, a sweet alcoholic drink produced from the African Marula tree I slept wonderfully and peacefully sleep that night.

The following day, I went to visit Edda and Karl by myself. They had invited me for coffee and cake and dinner. Irene stayed with my mother. They got along very well, and my mother was rather fond of Irene. It was a nice visit, with Edda and her husband, but as always, we got only a very short time to talk about Ottie and especially Irene and when we would meet. I did not feel good about being so deceptive, but that was how it was supposed to be. We told Karl that Edda and I would meet on the following Saturday morning to do a little shopping together. He did not mind and thus it was set.

I was a little nervous driving with Irene to Bad Kreuznach three days later. It was a nice and unseasonably sunny and warm day. Irene enjoyed the landscape and seemed to not be nervous at all. I wished I could tell what was going on in her mind. She was a fascinating woman. She married Ottie twelve years earlier, and she did not mind at all that he had all those children from different women, and that we were about to meet my birth mother. I admired her tolerance. On the other hand, Irene was right. This all happened long before she was born. There was nothing really strange about this. She liked me, I liked her, and Ottie loved her.

Edda and I decided to meet in town in the pedestrian zone, a street with one store next to each other and where cars are not allowed. After Irene and I parked the car in a parking garage, we went to the appointed place. At first I could not see Edda, but then I spotted her in the crowd of people crossing the street into the pedestrian area. We walked towards her. I hugged Edda and then introduced Irene. Irene and Edda hugged as well, and since Irene spoke German, there was no awkward translating. That was really an advantage. Irene told Edda how nice it was to finally meet her, and Edda returned the compliment. We stood there in the sun talking a little, when Edda unexpectedly proposed to go meet her sister.

I was stunned to say the least. I could not believe it, not only would I meet the first person from Edda's family, I would even bring Irene along. Editha, Edda's sister, as you might recall, knew about my existence and Edda lived with her during the last part of her pregnancy. Karl, of course, could never know about this meeting. So the three of us made our way through town to Editha's home. It was a fifteen-minute walk, during which we had a nice but not very deep conversation. It was more Edda and Irene who talked while I was in some sort of a trance, in disbelief of reality. The part of town where Editha and her husband lived was older, maybe from the 40s. Her rented house was a duplex, with three stories and a small garden in the back. We rang the doorbell and waited. Edda was not sure if her sister would be at home, but it was worth a try. She really wanted me to meet my aunt, and this was the chance to do it without Karl knowing.

A lady, who looked as if she were in her mid 70s, wearing a red sweatpants and a red sweatshirt opened the door. Her little twinkly eyes sparkled as she immediately realized who I was.

"What a wonderful surprise," she said. "Let me give you a big hug and a kiss!"

And that is what she did. I immediately was taken by this bubbly, energetic woman who had grey-blond short thick hair and blue eyes. Her skin was unbelievably smooth for her age, and with incredible agility she led us into the house and into the living/dining room to the left of the hallways. Then she basically ran into the kitchen at the end of the hallway to bring us something to drink. She wanted to open champagne for the event, but I had to drive and thus I had to refuse. Aunt Editha was so sparkly and so honest, I could not believe it. She told me that she could not understand why Karl made such a big secret with my heritage, and she would not do that. Irene, she also hugged and kissed once they were formally introduced. She thought that the whole thing was just the greatest. After all this secrecy with Karl, her openness and spontaneity impressed me, and I understood now why my sisters and Edda kept comparing me with her. It was an honor. Editha told me that the last time she "saw" me I was still in Edda's belly, and she kept hugging me to make up for all the lost time. The time with her was way too short, and Edda had to go back home. So we left Editha, promising to keep in contact from now on. We also took some very nice pictures of me with Edda and her.

Later on, Irene told me that she was glad that Edda expressed the wish to meet her. As a matter of fact, she found it flattering, and saw it as a compliment that Edda was willing to meet Ottie's wife. Irene told me that, with some of his other previous wives, she experienced various forms of jealousy. Irene was hoping that she could be some sort of an advocate for Ottie, and maybe help Edda find closure through meeting her. Irene hoped to help Edda somewhat understand that Ottie was not as bad as she might think, and be some sort of mediator between Edda and Ottie. Edda and Ottie had not only the language barrier, but also a continued resentment for forty years. Irene told me that she had actually look forward to meeting Edda, since I had always talked so nicely and caring about her.

CHAPTER 19

And the Story Continues...

Like every year around this time, Edda wrote me a letter on December 2, the day that commemorates our first meeting, and thus the beginning of a new era. That day, in 2007, it had been eleven years! Jill, who had been brutally murdered, would be in her 30s now, I could not help but wonder how she would look now and what her life would be like. Thinking about her felt like a lightning bolt went through my heart, and I quickly tried to focus my thoughts on Edda again and our first meeting. How fast this time had passed. In her letter, Edda reminded me about all the things that happened thus far: I got married, had children, received my Ph.D., and met Ottie. I was thinking about all these events, and in a way, even though Edda did not have part in my childhood, she had been present for all those other really important events in my life. Edda came into my life when it was changing the most, and she received two grandchildren.

The winter of 2007/08 was long in Wisconsin, with a record snow of over 100 inches. One day, in January, Edda called. She does not call very often, and usually when she does, it is not good news. I could hear her voice choked up and I immediately thought of Karl and was hoping he was fine. Then Edda told me that her sister was taken to the hospital in an emergency. Her trachea burst, and she was in the intensive care unit. She was conscious, but had to be fed intravenously and could not talk. She was on breathing machines and other life-supporting instruments. This news caught me by surprise. I feared for Editha, who I had taken a liking to when I met her in November. Since then, we had exchanged two letters, and Edda and I talked about introducing her to Carmen and Sean during the upcoming summer vacation in Germany.

Early in February, however, Editha's condition worsened and everybody feared for her life. I sent her some pictures of the kids and I, and her husband brought them to her at the hospital. Edda took the train once a week to the 40-mile distant city to visit her sister in the hospital. She would sing her songs from their childhood and tell stories about their families. Edda told me again how much she had suffered that she never had the chance to do this with her brother because her sister-in-law told nobody that he was in the hospital and dying.

In the meantime, finally, Christine settled in her dream country Bosnia, and found a good job, after she got the official work permit. An article about her was even published in a Bosnian newspaper. I was very happy for her and proud too. I wished so much she could fulfill her dreams and live in the country she really loved. I had the feeling things were starting to get resolved. My sisters and I e-mail or call from time to time, if not frequently, the conversations were pleasant and without any conflict. This was the situation I had dreamed of, that in time we would be friends, with no unreal expectations of each other and fear the other one would not like the other; just a normal, caring relationship. Every relationship has its ups and downs, and I think we worked through our differences.

The next time Edda and I talked on the phone, which was also on a more regular basis now, I told her that I was glad she was my mother. She was so happy. It is still difficult for me to say "I love you," but I wanted to let her know that I really liked her and was glad I had inherited so many characteristics from her. Even my sisters had to agree that not only was I the one who looked the most like her, but I also had her character. That was a big compliment to me.

On May 7, a letter from Edda arrived. She had seen Editha last Thursday, just as every week, and brought her the picture Carmen had drawn for her. I had written a letter and Edda read it to her sister. She seemed happy about it, although she seemed not to be doing so well. She still could not speak, and her health had improved a little, but she was still supported by machines. That last week though, she had not been her usual self. She could barely stay awake for Edda's visit, and Edda told me that her skin looked pale and grayish. I had just finished reading the letter, when the telephone rang. It was Edda. I was excited and told her that I had just received her letter. Then I halted in my excitement because I suddenly sensed that something was wrong. In fact, I had the distinct feeling that Aunt Editha was no longer among us. I was right, she had died just one hour earlier. I felt sad, but at the same time, I knew that Editha was where she had wanted to be for quite some time. She was a strong woman, full of life, without fear of life or death. I knew that she was fine, as strange as this might sound. Sometimes I wonder about modern medicine and the inability of many humans to let go. I am not afraid of death, but of the pain I might have dying and the pain felt by the people I will leave behind. Especially when you have young children, you do not want to leave this world. I really liked Editha for the short time I knew her. She had a great personality; she was so happy and so full of life. She exercised in the fitness center three times a week, even at seventy-five years old, and was sure that some of the "younger" men there had an eye on her. Well, good for her, I can only say. She was so openly happy about me coming, and about Irene, she thought nothing about me bringing my birth father's wife to meet my birth mother and her sister. When I grow up, I want to be like her!

Edda was very sad that her sister would not get the chance to see my children this summer, something we planned to do. I am a little sad about this too. Edda concluded the call by saying I should tell everyone, which I took to be my mother and Ottie. So I did, I called my mother first and then Ottie. I started to say Edda called when he interrupted me and said,

"She wrote me a letter."

"She did?"

"Yes."

"She sent it to you?"

"Well, she sent it to Irene, but she always sends greetings to me too."

That is kind of what I thought. I told him then that Editha had died, and Ottie immediately wanted Irene to call Edda to express his condolences.

"No, you can't! But you could write and send the letter to one of her daughters."

Ottie told me that my sisters wanted to meet him. He told me that Edda put pictures of her, and her daughters, into the letter telling him their names and what they were doing. "Really? What is going on here," I was wondering. Ottie put the pictures of the four women into the same frame of the picture of him, Irene, us, and my siblings. He jokingly told Irene that those could be his daughters, if he and Edda would have married long ago. I replied:

"Things would probably be very different right now."

"Maybe not," he answered. He was right. Things were supposed to happen exactly as they had. And to be honest, I was grateful for that.

But I also realized at that moment how much Ottie and Edda needed to meet, and how much they actually wanted to see each other. There was still some unfinished business, some unanswered questions, which needed to be resolved for both of them to go on with their lives and to resolve their past. I knew that they needed to meet, no matter what. And if Edda would ever come visit again, I would arrange a meeting whether she wanted to or not. They had to get over the past and start a new beginning. I really admire Irene, who is so self-confident that she does not mind at all. She knows Ottie loves her and she also wants this thing to be resolved.

Twelve years earlier, I woke up in Tucson and decided to find my birth mother. I could never have imagined all the things that would happen on this path, and all the wonderful people I would meet. I could not have imagined the reactions of my parents, the generosity of my adopted family, and tolerance towards the search of my past. The past was not without stones, things were not always easy and decisions had to be made. However, I am so very grateful for everything and everyone I have encountered over the years. I am blessed to say that I have four wonderful families, and I would not want to miss them. Last Easter, the kids and I went to Kentucky with Monte to surprise my grandfather at his eightieth birthday. He was so surprised he jumped up from his chair, almost overthrowing the table. He told me he had asked my birth father that morning if he thought I would call that day. He could not have imagined I would actually come visit him on that special day. I am grateful I had that chance. Carmen and Sean, although still a little confused how all those people actually are related to me, have embraced their multiple grandparents and aunts and uncles, and are blessed with a huge loving family. My husband is a wonderful partner in my adventures, and patiently and openly embraces all new family members I might still find. I am not finished yet. I still have two brothers I have not found, and I would very much like to get in contact with them. I have not sufficiently explored my Cherokee heritage, of which I am particularly proud. And last, but not least, I would like Edda and Ottie to meet, at least one time, so they could talk with each other and put the past behind. I want them to start a new friendly and understanding relationship, without resentment or hate. That is my dream.

Epilogue

In the meantime I have found my brother Chad as well. He is a wonderful person with a lovely family and I feel blessed to count him to my expanding family as well.

I have also learned a lot more about myself. A very dear friend pointed out a very interesting fact.

> *"In a twisted way Karl and you seem to be held back by similar issues. He does not want other people to know about what connects you to his family to avoid hurting his family. You do not want him to be "Opa," avoiding hurting your family."*

How right she is. Reading her statement made me understand Karl and my situation much better. We both have found additional families, which we are fond of. However, we have our own families, we like to protect and keep intact.

Just as I had limits in my acceptance with not inviting Edda to our wedding or calling Karl "Opa," he does have the right, to keep me a "friend" of the family for the outside world. It does not at all effect the relationship we have together. In fact, in the past year Karl and I have developed a real nice relationship surrounding his illness. Karl is eager to accept Ross's advice concerning cancer treatment options, since this is Ross's passion and education. Even though Karl's health is fading, his spirits are up and I admire him for this.

German Almond Cake

Ingredients dough:

2 cups sour cream (about 1 big container or 450 grams)
2 cups sugar
2 eggs
1 teaspoon vanilla extract
3 cups of flour
1 tablespoon of baking powder

Ingredients topping:

2 packages of sliced almonds
1.5 sticks of butter (sweet, unsalted)
1 cup of sugar

Instructions:

Preheat the oven at 350 degrees Fahrenheit. Place the sour cream, sugar, eggs, and vanilla into a large mixing bowl and stir well. Add the flour and baking power and mix well. Grease a baking sheet and put dough into it, flatting the dough with a spatula. Bake for about 20 minutes.

In the meantime, in a small cooking pot on the stove heat the butter. Add the sugar and almonds. Stir well while cooking.

Take the cake out of the oven and add the almond paste evenly on the cake. Bake for another 10 minutes.

Enjoy!

About the Author

Photograph by Bill Livick, Editor, Oregon Observer

Julia Isabell Meyers was born in Germany in 1968. At two months she was adopted by her loving parents and grew up with one younger brother in a small, picturesque German community.

After her high school graduation in 1987, Julia completed a two year apprenticeship at a local bank. Not being fulfilled with this profession, she began to study Cultural Anthropology at the University in Frankfurt, Germany and graduated with a Masters Degree in 1995.

In the meantime she had found her love for Archaeology and for four years traveled throughout the world excavating in the American Southwest, Germany and the Andes of Argentina. In 1997 she was accepted at the Ph.D. program to the University of Arizona in Tucson, Arizona. There she met her husband Ross and they married in 1999 in Germany. The couple have two children: Carmen is ten and Sean is eight.

In 1996, Julia Meyers decided to search for her birth mother, who she met for the first time in December of the same year. In 2004, she then continued her search for her birth father, who had been an American soldier stationed in Germany. They met in December 2004. In 2005, when her husband Ross graduated with a Ph.D. from the University of Arizona, they relocated to the Midwest, where he was born and raised.

Julia finished her Ph.D. in 2007 and is now pursuing her career as a writer. Today Julia and her family are residing near Madison, Wisconsin.

Index

• N •